PENGUIN
BURNING

Deepti Priya Mehrotra's published works include *Gulab Bai: The Queen of Nautanki Theatre*, *Home Truths: Stories of Single Mothers*, *A Passion for Freedom: The Story of Kisanin Jaggi Devi*, *Western Philosophy and Indian Feminism*, *Ekal Maa* and *Bharatiya Mahila Andolan*. She is presently pursuing research on democratic-feminist social movements 1970s onward, as a Fellow with the Nehru Memorial Museum and Library, New Delhi. She has a PhD in political science, and a post-doctoral thesis in philosophy. Deepti remains actively involved with varied educational and social organizations, and has taught in Delhi University, her alma mater.

PRAISE FOR THE BOOK

'The book tells the moving story of how this very ordinary woman from a humble rural background has become an icon for human rights activists everywhere'—*The Hindu*

'Moving away from conventional forms of writing, Mehrotra brings to presence various unacknowledged acts and individuals, from scribbles of solidarity to voices of protest . . . Locating Sharmila's struggle in a glorious tradition of women's movements in Manipur and the deterioration of the same as a militarized space . . . the writer analyses the struggle in the Gandhian tradition of soul-force and non-violence, embodying a civilisational challenge against dominant paradigms of development, consumerism and mindless destruction of nature'—*Biblio*

BURNING BRIGHT

IROM SHARMILA AND THE
STRUGGLE FOR PEACE IN MANIPUR

Deepti Priya Mehrotra

PENGUIN BOOKS

An imprint of Penguin Random House

PENGUIN BOOKS

USA | Canada | UK | Ireland | Australia
New Zealand | India | South Africa | China

Penguin Books is part of the Penguin Random House group of companies
whose addresses can be found at global.penguinrandomhouse.com

Published by Penguin Random House India Pvt. Ltd
4th Floor, Capital Tower 1, MG Road,
Gurugram 122 002, Haryana, India

Penguin
Random House
India

First published by Penguin Books India 2009
This revised edition published 2015

Copyright © Deepti Priya Mehrotra 2009, 2015
Foreword copyright © Mahasweta Devi 2015

Back cover photo: Meira Paibis, literally women torch-bearers, protest against
AFSPAin 1980; courtesy Wairakpam Ningol Mangol

ISBN 9780143424659

Typeset in Bembo by SÜRYA, New Delhi

Printed at Repro India Limited

www.penguin.co.in

CONTENTS

ACKNOWLEDGEMENTS

I dedicate this book to my mother, Preetvanti Mehrotra, with deep gratitude. Although Ma passed away on 14 August 2007, her undying spirit is with me, with us. She loved earth and sky, flowers and poetry, theatre and art ... and pursued varied creative projects with enormous vitality, striving towards perfection in teaching, writing, dramatics, gardening, cooking, community work and much else. Incredibly generous, she encouraged me to travel to Manipur in April 2007, despite her own critical illness. She was a marvellous teller of dramatic tales, and whatever wisdom I have learnt, I learnt first from her.

To my mind, Irom Sharmila's spirit and my mother's are in some senses akin: they are ordinary persons passionate about preserving the innocence of the earth, caring enough to work hard and make sacrifices. For all that she is and all that she represents, I thank Sharmila. I also bear a debt of gratitude to Sharmila's grandmother Irom Tonsija Devi (1903–2008), her mother Shakhi Devi and numerous other Imas (mothers or elderly women activists).

I thank Sunandita, my daughter, for her love and patience, as well as for travelling with me along much of the way. I thank my father, Ram Narain Mehrotra, for his warm and steady interest in my welfare and my endeavours, and for the inspiration he provides.

I am grateful to all the Manipuri peacemakers, activists, thinkers and friends—for answering endless questions and helping me understand their world from different angles. I hope the book does some justice to the trust they reposed in me. At the same time I make no claim to expertise, and the inadequacies that remain are entirely my own.

I am grateful to close friends, family members, colleagues and students, for their varied and extremely valuable support.

Many thanks to Ravi Singh, who backed the idea of this book from the moment I proposed it, Kiran Sahni for her enthusiastic reading, Paloma Dutta for her meticulous editing, Chiki Sarkar for backing a second edition, and the rest of the production team for providing all-important final touches.

FOREWORD

Deepti's book on Irom Sharmila is being reprinted. I feel very happy and proud to hear this. The story of Irom Sharmila is the story of Manipur. For me, and many persons like me, it is Sharmila who represents Manipur. I fully believe that this book will reach countless readers, in our country and in many countries of the world, just as my books have reached.

I myself have translated this book into Bengali, with one collaborator. I did it as a labour of love. Nobody asked me to do it. The book is called, *Banhiman Jiban: Irom Sharmila Ebong Manipurer Shanti Andolan.* I saw to its publication with Dey's Publishing, the best Bengali language publishing house. It was published in 2011 and has already reached Bengali readers. My hope is that the book will be translated into Malayalam, Telugu, Gujarati, Marathi and French, Spanish, German, Italian and other languages of the world, just as my books have been, so that the story of Irom Sharmila travels and spreads far and wide.

I believe that the twenty-first century is the century of Irom Sharmila.

The story of Irom Sharmila is the story of mother earth. That is why this story should reach all the regions and all the countries of the world.

Mahasweta Devi

(Adapted from Mahasweta Devi's Foreword to the Hindi book, Irom Sharmila aur Manipuri Janata ki Saahas Yatra, 2010)

PREFACE
THE IRON LADY OF MANIPUR

It is March 2007, and spring is in the air. Bees and butterflies hover around fragrant white flowers of the china orange tree next to my window. Kites and crows fly overhead, bulbuls and sparrows twitter near at hand, searching for safe places to nest. Fresh green shoots come up on the fern I thought was dead. All winter I have hardly watered the lawn, yet the grass is indescribably lovely. I think of Irom Sharmila Chanu, a tall slim woman, intelligent as can be—who became my friend during four winter months.

I write of her because I miss her. When I begin writing, she is no longer in Delhi; I can no longer reach her within half an hour. On 4 March 2007, she flew back to Imphal. I write of her because she is history in the flesh, being lived out in our times.

☖

Irom Sharmila, a young Manipuri, has been on indefinite fast since November 2000. She is fasting to protest the killing of innocent people by security forces meant to protect them. She is opposing the Armed Forces Special Powers Act

(AFSPA), a law promulgated to curb insurgency in the state. Under this law security personnel can shoot and arrest anybody, and raid premises, upon mere suspicion of insurgency. They often target ordinary people, misusing these special powers. Newspapers report innumerable incidents of false encounters. Human rights organizations have documented hundreds of cases of killing, arrest, rape and torture of innocent people.

People throughout Manipur live in a state of fear: on the one hand they fear insurgents, on the other hand security forces. A cycle of violence has been set up by these two groups. Caught in the crossfire, ordinary people in this beautiful state have lost all semblance of normal life. Rather than being an effective counter-insurgency measure, AFSPA is in fact encouraging growth of insurgency.

In November 2000, ten innocent people were mowed down by security forces in Malom, a village near Imphal. Irom Sharmila, who hails from a very ordinary family of Imphal, could not accept the situation. In response to this tragedy, she sat on hunger strike—her demand: withdrawal of AFSPA from Manipur. She refused to eat until and unless this draconian legislation was removed. Later in the same month the government arrested her, and began force-feeding her through a nasal tube. She has been released, and re-arrested, innumerable times since then. For over fourteen years now, she has stood by her demand, refusing to eat. She has spent most of these years alone in jail, in Imphal.

ॐ

I think of Irom Sharmila's sensitive eyes, questioning look, and a delighted smile waiting to break out. Yet her sorrow is pervasive, deep. With wisdom beyond her years, she decided to act—an original move aimed at changing, against all odds, the course of history.

At the age of forty-three, she is a name to reckon with. Newspapers and journals have dubbed her 'The Defiant Lady', 'The Iron Lady of Manipur', 'youth icon', 'a satyagrahi' and 'an Unlikely Outlaw'. One individual, she has taken on the might of the state.

Ordinary people rally around Irom Sharmila. She draws power from her unwavering resolve. Her commitment is total, her will strong as steel. She says, 'I am doing my bounden duty ... I am a rational being, acting on my conscience.'

ॐ

When I first met her, on 5 November 2006, I did not know I would one day write about her. I was unaware that she has so many words to share. I went simply to pay homage to a person of great courage, who had been on indefinite political fast for an unbelievable six years.

The previous day, an email, marked 'Action Alert', arrived in my inbox, sent by one Onil K., diverted to me by a colleague in Delhi University. The Alert read, '... We are looking for female volunteers to stay with her for a minute or hour or day or night as a kind gesture to show support to her non-violent movement. Presently she is in Delhi, AIIMS hospital, New Private Ward, Room # 57, under police custody charged under section 309: attempt to commit suicide. Only one female is allowed to stay with her by the police. She is quite alone in the hospital under police surveillance and still not giving up the fight.'

I imagined her weak, lying down, turned towards the wall, with barely any energy left. But I found her filled with vitality—self-illuminated. She was keen to converse and talked about many things. She related how she had flown from Imphal to New Delhi after being released from jail (in Imphal) on 3 October 2006. She recounted her experiences while in New Delhi.

Several weeks later, after she and I had met many times, I told her I would, someday, like to write about her. She smiled indulgently. She had just read a short account about a peasant freedom fighter called Jaggi Devi, and felt a sense of resonance with that passionate crusader.[1] She urged, 'You must write a book. A book has a lot of power. If it is a good book, more and more people will read it. It will be in the libraries. People will read it for research. Writing a book is very important.'

Later I go to Imphal to meet her; she is kept in judicial detention, in virtual solitary confinement, and force-fed. I meet her family, in their village on the outskirts of the city: her mother Shakhi Devi, grandmother Tonsija Devi, brothers and sisters, aunts and uncles, nieces and nephews. There is her wider family too—human rights activists, lawyers and ordinary people. A scooter-rickshaw driver is reluctant when I ask him to take me to Kongpal Kongkham Leikai, but when I add it is Irom Sharmila's family I'm heading towards, he sparkles with readiness. 'Sharmila Didi!' he intones with wonder and pure affection.

ॐ

Her struggle touches and connects, in its stark simplicity, with common citizens, and not just in Manipur. Thoiba, a research scholar in Delhi University, muses, 'Sister has now become the sister of everybody in the world.' Radha, an undergraduate in the same university, confides, 'After meeting her, for the first time I feel proud to be an Indian.'

Sharmila represents, and in many ways *is*, the ordinary person. This is precisely what makes her extraordinary. She speaks for many whose voices fade into oblivion, routinely unheard. In the present era of ruthless maldevelopment, militarization and abuse of power under guise of democracy and welfare, she stands for honest truths, stark and unadorned.

Her stand reiterates, in an idiom quite different from the academic or technical, the importance of human dignity, freedom and cultural integrity, and poses what is in essence a civilizational challenge. The direct arena is political, but the challenge is posed at multiple levels.

ༀ

Irom Sharmila's fast has stretched over fourteen years, and may carry on for many more. Her protest is an uncompromising call to the conscience. Authorities dub her a 'habitual offender', arresting her for attempted suicide. They know it is a false charge, for Irom Sharmila is not fasting unto death. Rather, she is fasting unto life, to remove a brutal law that allows the murder of innocent people.

She will neither compromise, nor give up the fight halfway. In staking a claim to peace as a basic right due to all people, she has become a symbol, an icon and an inspiration. The symbolism is powerful in its surrealism. The everyday mixes with the exceptional, the imagined with the unimaginable. She is down-to-earth and matter-of-fact, yet her act of daring is, literally, unthinkable for the rest of us. Her chosen path is original, uncompromising and very tough.

She has decided to sacrifice 'normal' life for the sake of a higher cause. By refusing to accept status quo, compromise and *get on with life*, she has redefined the 'normal'. Her sacrifice speaks louder than words, insisting: It is not normal for ordinary people to be killed in the name of law and order. It is not normal for us to look the other way. When innocent people are killed in the name of justice by a state that claims to be a democracy, it is *not* normal to ignore the violations, and just get on with one's own life.

She lives close to the bone, as close to her beliefs and convictions as is humanly possible. By withdrawing from the natural activity of eating food, she draws attention to her reasons. We understand that she refuses to condone abnormal levels of violence, and pretend that all is well with the world. She allows her deepest aspirations to guide her decisions, and organize her life. As such, she has become an abiding inspiration. She stakes no claim to being a yogi or a saint: she is a mere mortal, like any of us.

Her fast, which is entirely her own decision, is a powerful way of reclaiming agency. She emphasizes it is the only means at her command, since she lacks economic or political power. Others may not be able, or really want, to follow her way. Nevertheless, her action stirs us into reflecting on how we too may recognize, and express, our deepest concerns, articulate what we think is normal, and indeed the obverse too: what we, as sane human beings, find abnormal, objectionable and unacceptable.

Gazing at billboards in an American market, a Buddhist monk remarked, 'They are trying to steal my mind.' 'They' thrive on profit, produce weapons of mass destruction, overuse the earth's resources, dispossess the poor, and manipulate our minds and bodies. Artificial wants are created, subliminally; we become obsessed with *things*, distracted from living out our beliefs, honing our minds. Like automatons we work to earn, spend and keep the systems running smoothly. Corporations and nation states defend a gargantuan military–industrial complex against people's dissent and questioning. States defend boundaries and Gross National Products rather than citizens' lives, homes and hearths. Militarized nation states often violate, rather than protect, the vulnerable. They threaten human survival, destroying what is beautiful and innocent. In the name of security, insecurity is bred.

Those who dissent might themselves take up guns, like cornered rats attacking in defence, using sharp claws and killer teeth. Others, like Irom Sharmila, refuse to adopt the ways of the oppressor. They choose non-violence.

Such a choice requires that we pause, allow ourselves to step out of the logic of the gargantuan system, and develop the ability to be different, to be ourselves, to *be* the alternative. Non-violent resistance demands enormous mental and spiritual energy, as well as physical endurance. It is an active move, perhaps even a giant leap forward, for humanity.

PREFACE TO THE SECOND EDITION

Five years since its first publication, *Burning Bright* remains as relevant as it was when first published. Both Irom Sharmila as well as the state of Manipur seems to be suspended in time, caught in a complex web of human ideals and hard political realities.

This book has helped strengthen public interest, awareness and understanding of the situation in Manipur. Agatha Sangma, then a member of Parliament (Union Minister for State, Ministry of Rural Development), said at the launch of this book, (New Delhi, September 2009): 'I have great respect for Irom Sharmila. In my view, AFSPA should be withdrawn from Manipur.' Countless voices echo these sentiments, a groundswell that has grown with time.

The book has been used by social scientists and teachers, at school and university level; by human rights organizations, media-persons and women's movement activists.

In 2010, cultural activists and Gandhian thinkers from Kerala created a play on Sharmila, much of it based on this book, and performed it as a mission for peace, from Kerala to Imphal. S.V. Ojas, a young theatre artiste from Pune, subsequently performed the play hundreds of times, in different venues, as a powerful monoact. During November 2009, the book was launched a second time in Imphal, at the Festival of Hope, Peace and Justice, held annually to mark the day on which Sharmila began her fast. An anthology of Sharmila's songs was released during the same week, titled *Keishumshangee Rani*, i.e. 'Imprisoned Queen'. Documentaries were screened, plays staged, and a few hundred people undertook a one-day solidarity fast. Significantly, writer Mahasweta Devi was denied permission to meet Irom Sharmila.

A Chennai-based publisher took the initiative to translate *Burning Bright* and bring it out in Tamil (as *Irom Sharmila: Manipurin Irumbu Penmani*, 2010), even as Mahasweta Devi herself translated and oversaw publication in Bengali. A human rights group collaborated with a publisher to bring out a Hindi-language version, *Irom Sharmila aur Manipuri Janta ki Saahas Yatra*, which was launched in 2010 in Delhi by veteran Gandhian educationist Radha Bhatt, and human rights crusador Professor Manoranjan Mohanty. In Jaipur, the People's Union for Civil Liberties and Bhanwari Devi, courageous anti-rape activist, released the Hindi book a second time. There was a buzz around the book, and the reason for the buzz is the intense human interest that Sharmila's story evokes.

Vibrant public discussion was sparked off (2009–2014) around presentations based on the book, at venues as diverse as Police Academy, Jaipur; Mazdoor Kisan Shakti Sangathan, rural Rajasthan; Aligarh Muslim University; Delhi University's Regional Centre for Elementary Education; Jamia Millia Centre for North East Studies; Manipur Study Group, New Delhi; Institute for Comparative Human Rights, University of Connecticut; Kriti Peace Day celebrations; WISCOMP's Conflict Transformation Programme on 'Gender, Democracy and Transformation in South Asia'; Women's Feature Service,

ICRC Roundtable on 'Women in Conflict Zones'; seminar organized by South Asian Dialogues on Ecological Democracy; Zubaan and Heinrich Boll Stiftung's workshop on 'Cultures of Peace in North East India'; Control Arms Foundation India's workshop on 'Rewriting History'; among others.

Human rights organizations, ordinary citizens, artists, women's organizations, continue to lobby for repeal of the Act. Since 2010, the Save Sharmila Solidarity Campaign, encompassing over seventy civil society organizations, has held public demonstrations, lobbied with National Human Rights Commission, Prime Minister and President of India, urging repeal of AFSPA. In 2011, the Kashmir to Imphal People's Rally registered popular demand for removing AFSPA from the North-East and Jammu & Kashmir. A campaign 'From Gandhi to Sharmila' was initiated by Just Peace Foundation, in which youth from India, Korea and Hong Kong took part, along with the Asian Human Rights Commission.

In 2011, North-East Students' Organisation (NESO) members demonstrated with their mouths gagged, in Guwahati, demanding removal of AFSPA from the region. In December 2011, 'Artists Against AFSPA', including eminent artists Nalini Malani, Rekha Rodwittiya, Shilpa Gupta, Vasudha Thozur, Raqs Media Collective and several others, organized artwork, panel discussions, procession of flags created by artists, and screened documentaries on the subject, in support of Sharmila's cause, at Mumbai's National Gallery of Modern Art.

Every year during the first week of November, hundreds of people from all walks of life observe a token fast. In Manipur, student bodies like All Manipur Students' Union (AMSU), and civil society groups including All Manipur Kanba Ima

Lup (AMKIL), Sharmila Kanba Lup, Meira Paibis, and those affected by atrocities, take part. Some members of Manipur People's Party join. In Imphal, the venues of the mass hunger strike include the Ima Market in the heart of town, and the Jawaharlal Nehru Institute of Medical Sciences (JNIMS) inside which Sharmila is interred. Poetry recitals, street theatre, music, documentaries, and protest demonstrations have been held, along with one-day hunger strike, by thousands of people supporting Sharmila's cause—in cities like Delhi, Bangalore, Varanasi, Bhubaneswar, Kolkata, Guwahati, Chandigarh, Pune, Patna and Jaipur.

In January 2014, a Manipur People's Convention was held to strengthen the Repeal AFSPA Campaign, at Lamyanba Sanglen, Palace Compound, Imphal.

In January 2013, the Justice Verma Committee highlighted misuse of AFSPA by armed forces and recommended that sexual violence by men in uniform be brought within the purview of ordinary criminal law. In May 2013, UN Special Rapporteur on Extrajudicial, Summary or Arbitrary Executions recommended that AFSPA be repealed or at least reformed. However, Home Minister P. Chidambaram declared in the same year that, due to opposition from the Army, the Indian Union is unable to withdraw or even amend AFSPA.

In 2012 a PIL (public interest litigation) was filed in the Supreme Court of India, by Extra Judicial Executions Victims' Families Association, seeking justice for 1,590 cases of alleged extra-judicial killings and disappearances since the 1980s. A Special Investigation Team was set up and, on 8 August 2014, the Manipur government handed over a series of inquiry reports to the Supreme Court, detailing crimes allegedly committed by Army, CRPF and police commandos. The inquiries were conducted by serving and retired district judges. A report by M. Manoj Kumar Singh, District Judge, Imphal East, details the rape of a fifteen-year-old schoolgirl committed by two Army personnel of the 12th Grenadier on 4 October, 2005. The victim committed suicide the same day. Other crimes recorded include arbitrary killing of a mother singing her baby to sleep at home; a fifteen-year-old girl carrying lunch for her father to his workplace; spectators at a volleyball match; and so on. The report notes, '[Armed forces] think themselves placed at the elevated status of impunity by the legislation and think wrongly they are given license to do whatever they like . . .' The Justice Hegde Committee set up by the Supreme Court described AFSPA as 'a symbol of oppression, an object of hate and an instrument of discrimination and high-handedness'. The Committee noted that from the sample of cases considered, not a single encounter was genuine, and not a single victim had a terrorist background or even a criminal record.

The campaign for accountability and justice carries on, and many people think of Sharmila as its symbolic leader. In 2014, she was offered a seat by the Aam Aadmi Party (AAP), New Delhi, and also by the ruling Congress party in Manipur. She refused both, describing herself as a protestor, not a politician. She said, 'I don't want to enter politics. It is not necessary to be in politics to do something.' The same year, she submitted an application expressing her desire to vote in the Lok Sabha elections, but permission was not granted.

Despite her stature and growing public support for the cause, she is constantly harassed, on trial, and in jail. In March 2013, the Patiala House court, New Delhi, framed charges against her for attempting suicide in 2006 (when she was in Delhi), and put her on trial after she refused to plead guilty. She was flown in from Manipur by the government. She disclaimed any suicide attempt, and stated, 'I love life. I do not want to take my life. I want justice and peace. It is my demand to live as a human being!'

October 2013: the National Human Rights Commission (NHRC) issued a notice to the Manipur government, seeking immediate removal of arbitrary restrictions on access to Irom Sharmila. She must be allowed to receive visitors as do all people in judicial custody. There is no judicial mandate for the restrictions, which are a 'breach of India's obligations under international human rights standards and principles, and a grave violation of human rights'. The NHRC noted that the Commission has received complaints on the terms of Irom Sharmila's imprisonment, which have been deliberately made harsh because she is a human rights defender; and a prisoner of conscience. Unable to give a satisfactory reply to NHRC as to why she was rarely allowed visitors, the state government was compelled to relax the arbitrary restrictions and she could have better access to visitors.

May 2014: at another hearing at Patiala House court, Sharmila reiterated, 'I love my life very much and I am very eager to eat something, if I get an assurance that this undemocratic Act will be removed.' During this brief Delhi trip, where she was escorted by security and hospital staff from Manipur, she expressed a desire to meet newly elected Prime Minister, Narendra Modi, in order to influence him, but the wish was not granted. She left a letter for him, in which she wrote about the heart-rending condition of people in Manipur and requested repeal of AFSPA, and justice for people of the North-East. The letter received no reply.

On 19 August 2014, the District and Sessions Court, Manipur East, ordered Irom Sharmila's release, noting that the prosecution has not been able to substantiate the charge of attempted suicide. Amnesty International called the 'release of prisoner of conscience Irom Sharmila a moral victory' (20 August 2014). She continued her fast, living in a temporary shelter in Imphal amid several supporters. Thousands gathered to celebrate her freedom. However, barely 40 hours later, the promise of freedom was denied: Sharmila was re-arrested: a posse of policewomen forcibly dragged, held and physically picked her up, even as she screamed and wept—a scene telecast over national television (22 August, NDTV). Manipur's deputy chief minister, Gaikhangam Gangmei, announced that Sharmila has not been arrested, rather, 'We are taking care of her life . . .'

In fact it *was* an arrest—a brutal one at that. On 5 September and again 19 September, the Judicial Magistrate, Lamphelpat, remanded Irom Sharmila to further judicial custody. The government of Manipur, as in fact the Indian nation, has yet to explain why Sharmila is branded a criminal and jailed. An activist such as Sharmila may be brought to hospital and force-fed: there is no need to arrest and imprison her, if the sole intention is to keep her alive. In the 1990s, environmentalist Sunder Lal Bahuguna, fasting to protest the Tehri Dam in Uttarakhand, was picked up by the government and force-fed, in order to keep him alive; he was not arrested, nor imprisoned.

On 26 August 2014, hundreds of people took part in a mass rally and public meeting at Wangkhei Keithel, against 'torture and inhuman treatment of Irom Sharmila'.

On 29 August 2014, Sharmila Kunba Lup held a mass silent rally at Porompet, Imphal, against 'inhuman treatment of Irom Sharmila'.

On 11 September 2014, a silent sit-in protest was held in Imphal, women gagged to symbolize the silencing of popular voices; the protest was against '56 years of AFSPA': the date was dubbed 'the invisible 9/11'. (9/11 was the day AFSPA was promulgated in the North-East, in 1958.)

As a concession to intense public agitation, in 2012, AFSPA was removed from seven assembly constituencies—Wangkhei, Yaiskul, Thangmeiband, Uripok, Sagolband, Shingjamei and Khurai—all in Imphal municipality. However, the Act was renewed for all the rest of Manipur,

Between 2009 and 2014, the situation has not really improved. Sharmila continues to be imprisoned. Manipur continues to suffer atrocities, sanctioned under AFSPA. What Binalakshmi Nepram, founder of Manipuri Women Gun Survivors' Network, calls the 'little red book on Manipur, especially Manipuri women's struggles' continues to serve a purpose.

MURDER OF INNOCENTS

Around ten persons wait at Malom bus stop, each with a plan for the day. Malom: a lovely village a few kilometres from Imphal city, set like a jewel in the Imphal valley, surrounded by fields and faraway hills. It is the year 2000. There is tension in the air in Manipur, almost the entire state declared a 'Disturbed Area' since many years. But today there is no special cause for worry. The air is crisp, the winter sun pleasant.

An armoured vehicle, with security men in uniform, rifles cocked, zooms into view. The people at the bus stop keep waiting for their bus: they have no warning, none at all. Moments later, each of them feels a searing pain. Killer bullets penetrate their bodies, warm blood spurts. In a split second of stark awareness, each person realizes he is dying. Killed inexplicably: for no reason. By then, it is too late.

ॐ

A place called Malom near the Imphal airport witnessed cold-blooded killings of innocent people by the Assam Rifles. They shot at point blank range eight* people

---

*It was in fact *ten* persons: an inadvertent error

1

sitting at the bus stop in the usual garb of encounter with the insurgents.

This sadistic action was taken 'lawfully' under the draconian law of Armed Forces Special Powers Act. The moment this news spread, Irom Sharmila, a very common girl of Manipur, felt deep hurt inside her. She instantly declared fast unto death till this law is abolished ...

—Dr N. Vijay Lakshmi, Sociologist, Professor, Manipur, University, Imphal[2]

The ten killed in this encounter were simple persons going about their daily lives. They were not insurgents or militants. There was no evidence that any of them was ever involved in insurgency or anti-state activities. Five were residents of Malom village—twenty-seven-year-old S. Robinson Singh, seventeen-year-old S. Chandramani Singh, nineteen-year-old T. Shantikumar Singh, eighteen-year-old S. Prakash Singh and twenty-three-year-old Inaocha Singh. Fifty-year-old G. Bapu Sharma was from Lairenjam, thirty-five-year-old K. Bijoy Singh from Leimapokpam, sixty-year-old L. Sana Devi from Kabow Wakching, fifty-year-old O. Sanayaima Singh and thirty-four-year-old A. Raghumani Singh, from Nambol Naorem.

If a democratic state turns armed men loose upon a population, where are people to go for justice? Military and paramilitary forces have been sent to Manipur to quell insurgency, but finding it difficult to track down real insurgents, who dwell typically in thickly forested terrain, in frustration they often shoot at random. The law protects them, grants them impunity.

That morning, a bomb had exploded near Malom, at the 8th Assam Rifles camp. The explosion was engineered by unknown insurgents. Angry Assam Rifles personnel shot dead ten innocent people—a self-styled act of revenge.

The citizens of Malom were stunned. People from other parts of Manipur extended their sympathies. They put their resources together, and built a memorial for the ten martyrs during the next few months, inaugurating it on 2 November 2001, exactly a year after the massacre. They named it the 'Ten Innocents Park'. Its clean, fine lines are open to the elements, swept by the breeze, washed by the rain, protected by the watchful hills. The memorial honours those who died so tragically, but whose sacrifice helped draw attention to the cause of peace and justice.

ᛏ

When she heard of the massacre at Malom, Irom Sharmila, a twenty-eight-year-old resident of Imphal, took a unilateral decision: she would go on hunger strike, and continue until AFSPA, the draconian law, was repealed. She went to Malom on 5 November 2000 and began her fast. Her slight figure rapidly became a nucleus for collective protest.

THE MAKING OF AN ACTIVIST

Irom Sharmila was born on 14 March 1972. It was a year of hope and promise, for Manipur was granted statehood after a long-drawn struggle. Although it became a full-fledged state of India in January 1972, Manipur's problems did not come to an end.

The youngest of nine children, Sharmila was observant and thoughtful, and soon became an avid reader. She absorbed information through newspapers and books, grandmother's stories and animated family discussions. She learnt of the troubled legacy of her homeland, and felt tremors of the turbulence that had not died down.

After completing school in 1991, she tried her hand at shorthand, typing, tailoring and journalism. Gravitating towards social work and human rights organizations, she worked awhile with different groups, gaining exposure, experience and a fledgling understanding.

In September 2000, she applied for a month-long internship with Human Rights Alert (HRA), a small, highly respected human rights organization. She joined on 2 October, and spent the first week attending an orientation workshop on human rights. This helped her consolidate stray pieces of information and place the human rights situation within a global perspective. The picture grew clearer as she read and heard about various international protocols, UN conventions, India's own commitments and actual events on the ground.

Everyday, she cycled three or four kilometres from home to the HRA office at Kwakeithel Thiyam Leikai. During the second week of internship she continued studying to hone her skills in analysing the human rights situation in Manipur. She became part of the Preparatory Committee formed by HRA for an Independent People's Inquiry Commission into the impact of AFSPA in Manipur. The Inquiry, headed by Justice H. Suresh, former judge of the Bombay High Court, was scheduled to take place the same month.

Babloo Loitongbam, executive director, HRA, recalls, 'Sharmila was completely serious. She was the only intern who did not miss a single day of work. She would cycle in, right on time in the morning, and accompany the team wherever they went—often cycling behind their car. She became very dedicated to the team members.'

Apart from Justice Suresh, the People's Inquiry Commission team comprised Colin Gonsalves, Supreme Court advocate and director of Human Rights Law Network (HRLN), New Delhi, and Preeti Verma, senior lawyer with the same organization. The Commission members made field visits during 21–26 October, interviewing a large number of victims of human rights violation, human rights defenders, lawyers, NGO workers, media persons and academics.

Sharmila listened to the team's discussions, and helped facilitate the deliberations. Because of her dedication and regular presence at all field visits, victims' testimonies and discussions, she gained enormously. It was an intensive exposure, packed into a tight time schedule. Sharmila was moved to the very edge of her endurance, particularly when she met victims of arbitrary action by the armed forces, and heard their experiences.

Sharmila learnt a lot from the team members too, and grew fond of them, especially of Preeti. She would often cook a special vegetable curry, and bring it to office to share with everybody there.

Within a few days, the team completed its investigations, and departed. But the experience left Sharmila somewhat changed. She was very charged up. Having encountered a great deal of shock and trauma, she was grieving and angry. She wanted to find a way to block the avalanche of violence hurtling all around, like boulders threatening to crush humanity.

Sharmila was completely serious. She would not miss a single day of work. She would cycle her route on time in the morning, and accompany the team wherever they went, often cycling behind their car. She became very

ॐ

On 2 November, just a couple of days after her internship with Human Rights Alert ended, she attended a seminar on 'Internal Cultural Peace' at Shangaiprou, Ghari. She cycled to the venue, a few kilometres from her home in Imphal. It was a Thursday, the day on which she kept a fast. She had been keeping a regular weekly fast for many years.

When she returned home from the seminar that evening, she heard news of the Malom massacre. Knowing that such arbitrary violence had become chronic in her state, she felt she had a responsibility to try to end it, somehow. She determined to do whatever she possibly could, to restore peace. She had participated in various shades of social action, but found them insufficient to meet the challenge. She sought something direct, and irrefutable.

The idea of an indefinite fast had been knocking about

in her mind. The method appealed to her. Non-violent dissent, rather than retaliatory violence, seemed the only choice for somebody who wished, from the bottom of her heart, for peace.

During the night of 2 November, Sharmila was extremely restless. She wrote on a piece of paper, '*What is the origin of peace and what will be the end?*' She tossed and turned, with her mind in turmoil. She wanted to get to the root of the problem, and take a firm, effective stand. She prepared to give her all for the cause. Finally she took her decision, and fell into a short, deep sleep.

On 3 November, a number of people and organizations raised their voices against the massacre at Malom. The entire state of Manipur was shaken by this latest atrocity. Government imposed curfew in several parts of the state. Roads and bazaars were deserted.

The next day, curfew was relaxed for a few hours. Sharmila picked up her cycle and furiously pedalled towards Malom with the intent of reaching the site of the killings. But several people en route stopped her and warned her not to go ahead. She returned home. Her mother had just brought in provisions and sweets from the market. Sharmila ate some food, then, overwrought and weeping, told her mother she would not eat any meals after this. Seeing her daughter in distress, yet not understanding the full import of her words, Shakhi Devi tried to soothe her, and asked her to rest.

Sharmila made a vow to herself: 'I will not eat until AFSPA is withdrawn from Manipur.' Thus in the privacy of her home, she launched the public fast that became, in time, an internationally recognized act of political protest.

On the morning of 5 November, a Sunday, she attended a Universal Youth Development Council (UYDC) meeting at Sagolband. She revealed her plan to undertake an indefinite fast against the atrocities of the armed forces. Office bearers of this non-governmental civil society organization, including President Nilamani Kha-Nganba, Public Relations Officer G. Binarani Devi and Publicity Secretary N. Ranjit Singh, were concerned about such an extreme step, and tried to dissuade her. But their appeals confronted a rock-like will. They advised her to seek her mother's blessings, secretly hoping her mother would dissuade her.

Returning home, Sharmila found her mother in the yard tending and cutting *maroi nakuppi* vegetable. She told her mother she had something important to convey, and asked her to come into the house. Sitting by her mother's side she said, 'Ima, I am going to do something for the whole nation. I want your blessings for this.' She bent and touched her mother's feet. Shakhi Devi trusted this serious, strong-minded daughter of hers. Although she had no intimation of the enormity of the action Sharmila was planning to take, she knew, whatever it was would be for the common good. She gave her wholehearted blessings and embraced her child with tears in her eyes. Sharmila consoled her, 'Don't worry, Ima. God is everywhere.'

Sharmila sought blessings from her elder brothers, again without revealing the specific action she contemplated. They blessed her unreservedly, although later Irom Singhjit, her third brother, fourteen years her elder, says, 'If I knew she was planning to go on hunger strike, I would have tried to dissuade her. We would all have done so. That is why she did not tell her plan exactly.'

Sharmila went to the HRA office, housed in two small rooms adjacent to Babloo Loitongbam's residence. She informed him and his wife Shachi, a political scientist, about her decision. Recalls Babloo some six years later, 'I remember Sharmila walked into this room, Shachi was feeding our little baby girl at that time. She walked in and announced what she planned to do, very simply and directly, just like that. I was stunned. Shachi and I were both stunned. There was nothing we could say or do. I asked her if she was sure, and she replied, "I am sure." ... After that there was no turning back. I little realized how important her act would become. In fact, it took over all our lives. It became so important over the next years, more important than even the Independent People's Inquiry Commission we'd just held.'

Sharmila returned to UYDC and informed colleagues that she had indeed obtained her mother's blessings. G. Binarani, a good friend of Sharmila, accompanied her by rickshaw to the residence of Ima Kombi, president of Poirei Leimarol Meira Paibi, a women's human rights organization. Ima Kombi gave her blessings and wholehearted support.

The same day, Sharmila went to Malom, accompanied by a number of Meira Paibi and human rights activists. There, at the site of the recent massacre, Sharmila continued her fast. It was now a public protest.

Her indefinite fast—in its fifteenth year now—has become a parable for our times.

GROWING YEARS

As a child, Irom Sharmila absorbed ways of life and thought traditional to Manipur, 'land of nine hills and a valley'. She learnt basic skills, and strong moral values. Her caring, closely knit family provided her with a sense of security and inner confidence.

Living in Kongpal Kongkham Leikai at the edge of Imphal city, Sharmila's home was one of a cluster opening out onto paddy fields, the sky and hills beyond. Family members worked together to cultivate paddy. Women grew vegetables and wove cloth, their wood-and-bamboo looms a prized possession. Her mother Shakhi Devi, or an elder sister, would sit on a wooden stool and work deftly, robust movements flowing into multi-hued *phi*, cloth, for *phanek*s and *inaphie*s.

Shakhi Devi was forty-four years old when she gave birth to Sharmila, her ninth child. She was too exhausted to feed the infant. A sibling would cuddle the hungry baby and take her to a wet nurse—a cousin, aunt or neighbour who was currently breastfeeding her own baby. The extended family of Iroms spread across the colony—a cluster of houses of varied shapes and sizes set at odd angles, each with a tiny yard, and a tree or two. Sharmila was nursed, literally, by a collectivity of Imas.

Her father, Irom Nanda Singh, held a job as veterinary attendant in the government veterinary department. Nanda Singh's great-great-great grandfather Irom Devaram migrated to this spot in the early nineteenth century, from village Irom Meijro, some ten kilometres away. He and his wife cultivated the land and built a modest mud-and-bamboo home. Devaram's son Irom Kodram, Kodram's son Irom Roton, Roton's son Irom Chouba, and Chouba's son Irom Modon Singh continued to live on the same spot. Modon Singh and his wife Tonsija Devi had three sons, of whom Nanda Singh was the eldest.

The lineage stemming from Irom Devaram expanded considerably, branching into several homes, varied degrees of relations living as neighbours. They form a community of Iroms. For children growing up here, the extended-family settlement provides immense security. Inevitably, tensions sometimes arise between members, yet they share strong bonds of common ancestry.

To date, Iroms from this settlement, as well as Irom Meijro and elsewhere, gather on a particular sacred day, at a certain temple, cook and eat together, and perform ancient rituals designed to bring peace to their ancestors. Through such shared rituals they seek to maintain continuity, cosmic balance and a faith that sustains human life.

Sharmila, being the youngest among five brothers and four sisters, played with Bijoyanti and Ajit who were just a little older than herself. Besides these two, she had many playmates in the neighbourhood. Her older siblings were busy with studies, agriculture and housework. The entire clan called her Memtombi, meaning 'the youngest one'.

Shakhi Devi nurtured this last child of her womb with

cow's milk, rice gruel and vegetable curries. She grew plenty of green vegetables in the kitchen garden, and kept poultry. Often she cooked fish, caught from ponds nearby, a valuable addition to the daily diet.

Nanda Singh and Shakhi Devi could just about read and write Meiteilon, but were keen to educate their children. After completing high school, the eldest sons Bijoy and Raghumani joined the veterinary department. The third son, Singhjit, went on to Uttar Pradesh for a BSc in agriculture at the Agricultural University, Hapur. The fourth son, Chandrajit, went to Chennai to do a BE (Electrical), while Ajit, the youngest son, stayed on in Imphal and joined the veterinary department.

Sharmila's sisters Gomati, Runayendi and Bijoyanti studied, and helped their mother with weaving and housework. They accompanied her to the market to buy yarn and sell fabric. When the kitchen garden yielded a surplus, they took these vegetables to the Ima (women's) market, to sell. After Gomati completed high school, she married and moved in with her in-laws in Hodam Leikai, Imphal West. Runayendi completed a BA, then married and settled in Uripok Tourangbam Leikai, Imphal West. Bijoyanti completed a BSc, and began looking for a job.

For several years, Bijoyanti was unable to find a job. Despite doing well in her studies and securing requisite qualifications, she remained unemployed. This was deeply disturbing to her, and Sharmila, just a couple of years younger, was affected by the situation. Sharmila later explains, 'It is not easy to find a job in Manipur. My sister studied yet could not find a job. She could not pay the bribe. There are only government jobs in Manipur, and a big bribe has to be paid. From where could she pay? For years she kept trying. Finally, she was appointed as a Home Guard. This is the only kind of job there is. She was lucky to get it, after many years, without paying any bribe.'

Sharmila was a quiet, reflective child. Observing her brothers' and sisters' travails had a sobering effect on her. Bijoyanti did well in exams, yet underwent immense stress and frustration when hunting for a job. Singhjit and Chandrajit went outside Manipur for higher studies, completed professional courses and returned, but could not locate steady jobs. Finally Chandrajit set himself up as a freelance electrician, while Singhjit joined the Citizens' Volunteer Training Centre (CVTC), an NGO in Imphal, as agricultural officer.

Sharmila studied up to Class 5 in Khanglabung Child Centre, Soibam Leikai, and Classes 6–10 at Ananda Singh Higher Secondary School, Nongmeibung. She found her school studies very onerous. The older she grew, the more difficult it became to cope with the heavy, meaningless courses. Not a whiff of real life emanated from them: none of the drama she sensed around her, which even the daily newspapers hinted at. She hated the impersonal, drab, bloodless histories that were supposed to educate her. She was keen to understand the world around her, its politics and history, but her textbooks offered no illumination.

Alienated and disconnected from formal studies, her performance was lackadaisical. She failed in her first attempt at the Class 10 examination. 'That was the first failure in my life,' she recalls. She felt awful, but Shakhi Devi consoled her.

'Try again,' she said, philosophically. 'Don't give up!'

In 1989, when Sharmila was still in school, Nanda Singh contracted blood cancer, and passed away within a few months. With only Bijoy and Raghumani holding jobs at that time, the family was in dire straits. Since Nanda Singh had died in harness, his youngest son, Ajit, took up his job. Shakhi Devi, devastated by her husband's untimely death, moved in with Bijoy and his wife.

Sharmila also moved with her mother, to Bijoy's home. Their grandmother Tonsija Devi moved in with her second son, Irom Manglem Singh, and his wife Ibemhal Devi.

Sharmila did all she could to help her mother. At the same time, she tried to cope with her studies. She would plunge into her textbooks, but her mind wandered. When her textbooks taught the Indian Constitution, she questioned whether democracy was a reality in India. She read of India's freedom struggle and Gandhi's political activities with avid interest, but wondered why there was hardly any mention of the north-eastern states. Were they, or were they not, integral parts of India? Interested in significant issues and big questions, she was impatient with dry facts and stilted analyses. Lessons on India's development made her sit up and ask why, if India had built up massive infrastructure since 1947, so little of it was evident in Imphal. Why was there was so much poverty, illiteracy, unemployment and disease? Stereotypical answers failed to convince her—and the school system offered little more.

Sharmila devoured contemporary literature of all kinds, including political pamphlets. She possessed a lively mind, and was thirsty for knowledge. She loved the lilt and rhythm of poetry, and the drama and colour of mythology. She recalls later, 'I thought of the textbook as my enemy. It was never interesting for me. I was always very interested in society, what is happening around me. I was always interested in politics.' She had information, and many ideas stirred within her. But the formal system afforded no scope for expression. She continued her explorations into life, keeping eyes and ears open, listening to discussions raging in her family and neighbourhood, and puzzling over all the information and ideas. Introspective and thoughtful, she would mull over problems, and devise imaginary solutions. Soon she began participating in discussions, suggesting a different point of view, or simply asking a deeper question.

She heard of insurgency spreading all over the state, and knew of people in her neighbourhood who were rumoured to be in touch with insurgent groups. Sharmila followed the news about insurgents, often splashed in daily newspapers, trying to understand how the groups functioned, and what this meant for society. All this was fertile ground for an adolescent's imagination.

As for the Class 10 exam, she managed to clear it in her third attempt. For intermediate studies, she moved to Ibotonsana Girls Higher Secondary School, Uripok. She enjoyed cycling daily, for she saw and learnt much on the way. But the senior secondary textbooks were worse than ever: fat tomes, stuffed with meaningless information, couched in stilted language. She tried hard to mug up her lessons, because she wanted to do well. However, she failed the Class 12 exam.

This was a difficult phase in Sharmila's life. Her family was in turmoil due to Nanda Singh's death. Sharmila depended on her eldest brother for financial support. Aware that he had his own family to look after, she was keen to start earning her living.

She pushed herself to learn vocational skills. She became proficient at typing and shorthand. She went in for a course in tailoring. Although she had little interest in this, she did well enough. But her half-hearted efforts to land a job in these fields drew a blank.

She joined a course in journalism, and here her hidden talent emerged. Soon she began writing articles, even a column for *Huyen Lanpao*, a local newspaper. Equally significant, and unforeseen, was the flood of poems that began flowing from her pen. She wrote an occasional diary too—pages of prose, interspersed with sheer poetry.

Writing poetry brought her in touch with a deeper part of the self, and helped unlock subconscious feelings. There was some tension between various aspects of her life: poetry helped bridge the gaps. She began to develop a new sense of balance.

She was different from most youngsters around her. She had many friends, but kept aloof. A brooding intensity marked her apart. As she wrote poetry, she grew confident, came out of her shell, and made diverse connections with people.

❦

As an ordinary citizen, Sharmila experienced privation in this neglected state, far removed from the national capital. Manipur was removed not only physically from New Delhi, but also mentally and culturally. She saw how neglected her people were. She felt the daily humiliation of young rikshaw drivers, graduates with no other source of income, faces wrapped in cloth to hide their identities. People suffered acute unemployment, poverty and disease, lack of shelter and basic amenities. She grew critical of politicians, and the attitude of the Centre. What good was a development that did not benefit, or even reach, people?

Sharmila was convinced that nature cares and provides for everybody, just as a mother cares and nurtures all her children. Yet human beings, disregarding nature's ways, were setting up alien modes of production and consumption. She questioned the economic system that generated problems, and the political system that made matters worse.

In 1995, Sharmila's eldest brother Bijoy died—a cruel blow to the Irom family. Shakhi Devi and Sharmila moved in with Singhjit and his family. Singhjit worked at CVTC, on issues of local agriculture and livelihoods, while his wife Shanti supplemented the household income through weaving. They had three children—a daughter and two sons.

Sharmila continued exploring options for meaningful work. For a while she volunteered with CVTC. But rather than join any organization on a full-time basis, she kept seeking further. She became publicity secretary at the Blind School for Children at Takyel, Imphal West. She agreed to be assistant secretary of UYDC, and associated actively with the Manipur International Youth Centre. She attended workshops and seminars, travelling and gaining first-hand knowledge of life in different parts of Manipur.

She grew increasingly concerned about daily news of violence by insurgents, as well as by armed forces. She came across heavily armed men in jeeps, or positioned in busy markets, haranguing women or manhandling young men. She read of encounters in which security forces raided villages, shot people and made arrests. Wherever she went, she heard rumblings of discontent and anger, complaints about arbitrary arrests and brutality. She was very disturbed at the thought of ordinary people being violated, their lives destroyed.

From the mid-'90s onwards, Sharmila grew particularly interested in human rights, and issues of peace, justice and development. She learnt a great deal from senior colleagues in the field. She noticed that organizations were low on funds, yet committed to ambitious agendas. The political environment was hostile: on the one hand government agencies tried to harass, co-opt or crush independent organizations, and on the other insurgent groups often issued threats or indulged in open harassment. She realized that the work done by civil society organizations is difficult and demanding, and creates its own stresses and tensions. She sought ways to contribute to the tasks at hand. However, she remained troubled and dissatisfied, and felt convinced that something more was needed, to tip the scales.

In 1998 Sharmila attended a course in nature cure, a subject that fascinated her. As part of the course she learnt yoga, and began practising it daily. Some years later, she explains, 'I began doing yogasanas in 1998. My guru was in Imphal, a lady who taught me in 1998–9. After that, I do yogasanas every day.'

༓

After I get to know Sharmila, I try to understand the sources of her exceptional courage. Her childhood was spent in an ordinary family, but somehow the seeds of activism were sown within her, early on.

'Whatever we have learnt, we have learnt from our grandmother,' exclaims her brother Singhjit one day, in partial answer to my queries. 'All our strength is from our grandmother. Sharmila's strength is from our grandmother.'

He continues emphatically, 'Our grandmother taught us what is important. She would say, "If you find a gold coin on the road, it is like mud to you. Do not touch it. It is not yours. Do not pick it." To this day, we never pick anything we find. We never steal anything, big or small.' After a moment's reflection, he adds, 'Our grandmother told us, "Even if you have nothing, you can always give a smile. When you meet somebody, give a smile to the person." So that is why you will find we are always happy when somebody comes, we always greet every person with a smile ... Our grandmother told us the family history, the names of our ancestors—she said we must know this ...'

Grandmother Tonsija Devi had a sense of history, and it was not limited to family history. She carried memories of people's resistance to imperialism, as fresh as if the events had occurred yesterday. She herself participated in the Second Nupilan or Women's War of 1939—one of the major anti-colonial struggles in Manipuri history.

Over the years, Tonsija Devi recounted wonderful stories to her grandchildren—tales of modern resistance, as well as narratives redolent with ancient glory. As a child, Sharmila was enthralled by these stories; they fired her imagination.

Later she got to know many women who took part in people's movements, often as leaders. During the 1990s, she became well acquainted with a number of Meira Paibis, elderly women activists who have determinedly confronted a range of social issues since the '70s. She had met Meira Paibis in her locality since her schooldays, and heard of their struggles throughout the state. In the '90s, she joined Meira Paibi groups in their campaigns and discussions, benefiting greatly from their experience and wisdom.

Thus although her fast is a very individual act, it is born out of a bedrock of shared convictions, and collective actions. In this sense, it is the product of decades—nay, centuries—of history.

INHERITANCE: ANCIENT GLORY

Irom Sharmila carries Manipur within her. The rich culture of this ancient land has profoundly influenced her. She refers frequently to 'my homeland', 'my birthplace' or 'the very place of my birth', with fierce pride and protectiveness.

It is easy, when in Manipur, to imagine it as a whole world—self-contained, a state apart. Imphal valley, with the capital city at its centre, is surrounded, in what seems to be a perfect circle, by distant hills. A child might grow up here thinking of the world as an enormous bowl—filled, periodically, with rice!

For most people in 'mainland' India, north-eastern states are shrouded in mystery. After I made a trip to Imphal, more than one Delhiite asked me, 'Where's that?' and began raving about headhunters, terrorists and dog-eaters. Educated and illiterate seem alike in their ignorance. National-level social science textbooks are virtually blank on this region.

This fairy-tale region was a sovereign kingdom for nearly two millennia. Independent and proud, peace-loving yet steeped in ancient lore about warriors defending the kingdom, Manipuris are uneasy about being reduced to a tiny, neglected fragment of the Indian nation. They harbour a simmering discontent, memories of past glory adding fuel to the fire.

Ancient lore of this land flowed into Sharmila's being. Tonsija

Devi made Manipur's history come alive. She charmed the little girl with tales of kings and queens, gods and goddesses, and the dramatic deeds of ordinary people.

Tonsija told Sharmila that Manipur was once called 'Sana Leibek' or gold country, a land of blessed existence. It had an unbroken dynastic line, the Ningthoujous who reigned from AD 33, right up to 1891. The first king and queen, Nongda Lairen Pakhangba and Leima Leisna, established Kangla, in Imphal valley, as their capital. Tonsija related, 'Queen Leima Leisna was a Maibi, a priestess. She married Pakhangba. Leima Leisna and her brother, Chingkhong Poireton, came from a subterranean region in the east, with the rest of the Poirei tribe. Leima Leisna brought two hundred varieties of vegetables and fruits with her—a hundred meant to be cooked, and a hundred meant to be eaten raw. Poireton brought fire to Manipur, for the first time. This first fire still burns at Andro village, in Imphal valley.'

Later, the Poireis came to be known as Meiteis, literally fire-bringers. Even today, most Meitei families keep a fire burning in the 'phunga' or fireplace, at a prominent place in their homes.

Tonsija Devi related myths of common origin, like the Mao Maram legend: 'In the beginning was a woman Dziilo Mosiiro at a place called Makhel. One day she was sitting at the foot of a banyan tree. The spirit of Oramei (God) appeared in the form of a cloud and overshadowed her. She conceived. She had three sons—Ora (God), Okeh (tiger) and Omei (man). Later Ora and Okeh migrated to different places. Omei had three sons—Choutou, Alappha and Khephio. Choutou fathered the Meiteis. Alappha fathered the Kolamei, and Khephio the Nagas. Later, the Meiteis settled at Chingmeirong, near Kangla.'

Meiteis, the majority community, inhabit the valley, while other ethnic groups by and large dwell in the hill areas. Today there are some thirty-three or so ethnic groups including Anal, Chiru, Chongthu, Chothe, Gangte, Guite, Hmar, Kabui, Kharam, Khoibu, Khongjai, Koirent, Kom, Lamgang, Liangmei, Lushai, Mao, Maram, Maring, Mate, Tangkhul, Thougal, Thoudou, Vaiphei and Zemi. Most tribes have been classified into Naga or Kuki-Chin, which are broad groupings.

Meitei kings wielded power at the centre, but in some hill regions, other groups were powerful. The Meitei monarchy consolidated its dominant position through force and ritual. During coronation ceremonies, Meitei kings wore Naga robes. The possibility of peaceful coexistence was conveyed by popular legends such as the stirring romance between Panthoibi, a Meitei maiden, and Chingsomba, a Tangkhul Naga youth. According to legend, Panthoibi and Chingsomba faced many travails and hardships, but were finally united in marriage.

Manipuri children learn the story of civilization through participation in Lai Haraoba, the most important festival of the year, celebrated in every village and city street. Maibis and Maibas (traditional priests—female and male) dressed in striking red and white costumes, lead the dance, enacting the story of cosmic creation. With stylized gestures, they mime the creation of each part of the human body, beginning with the navel, moulding nearly a hundred body parts, to make a whole person. They go on to mime the equally intricate steps involved in weaving cloth, cultivating paddy and constructing a mud-and-bamboo dwelling. Children inherit, willy-nilly, a deep reverence for nature, as well as human art and ingenuity.

People honour seven fairy ancestors, the Lamleima taret, during Lai Haraoba. These include Phoubi, goddess of paddy, who is reputed to have travelled through the state, spreading the art of cultivation. She halted at a number of places, at each spot taking a husband, whom she left behind when she continued on her journey. After dying, she transformed herself into a paddy plant. Thus even in death, symbolically she gave birth to life. All the fairy ancestors transformed themselves into items of food and drink, marking the start of human civilization.[3]

Like every other Meitei child, Irom Sharmila learnt the story of genesis. Sidabi, the female godhead and Sidaba, the male, had two sons, Pakhangba and Sanamahi. Sidabi favoured the younger son Pakhangba, and took his side when there was a struggle for the throne. However, Sidaba favoured the older son, Sanamahi. In the end, Sanamahi won. From then on, he got enshrined in every family home.[4] His mother, Sidabi, is enshrined with him, but is considered less important. The female principle lost out, and was subsumed under the male principle. Sanamahism, the ancient religion of the Meiteis, is named after its central hero, Sanamahi.

The first historical ruler of Manipur, Nongda Lairen Pakhangba, had no knowledge of his father, but his mother's lineage was well known. He assumed the title Pakhangba to link his name with the mythical ruler-god by the same name. Pakhangba means, literally, 'one who knows his father'.

To date, most Meitei families install Sanamahi in their homes, and worship him daily. So it was in the Irom home. Every child knows that Sanamahi rules the inner world while Pakhangba, symbolized as a dragon-headed serpent, rules the external realm. The Pakhangba symbol, ubiquitous in

Manipur, is seen in a thousand different formations—one or many dragon-headed serpents, entwined in an endless stream of marvellous patterns.

Mythological and divine beings tend to inhabit the imagination of children and adults alike—Soraren the god of rain, Thongaren the god of death, Meitrang the god of fire, Panthoibi, Lairembi, Nongbok Ningthou, Wangburen, Sambubi and so on. Sanamahism is an animistic faith, closely resembling Vedic nature worship. Little Sharmila saw people around her praying, appealing for intervention in times of crises, worshipping forces residing in rocks, rivers and trees. To an impressionable child, the scores of colourful gods and goddesses seemed to be living entities, dramatic and powerful.

ॐ

A shrine to Shri Krishna enjoyed pride of place in the courtyard of Sharmila's childhood home. She was fascinated by her grandmother's morning routine, which culminated at the shrine. After a bath, Tonsija Devi would don spotlessly clean cotton clothing, paint a long vertical sandalwood paste tilak on her forehead and down the bridge of her nose, water the tulsi plant in the yard, and pay obeisance to Radha and Krishna. Krishna-bhakti co-existed with her strong belief in Sanamahism. There seemed no contradiction in embracing both faiths, and thus it was with very many people in the state of Manipur.

The Irom family reposed faith in Vaishnavite gods and rituals, and worshipped Sanamahi, as well as deities of sun and moon, agriculture and weaving. Sharmila often accompanied her mother and grandmother to the Krishna temple, a short walk away. She enjoyed the sound of chanting, and the incense, fragrant flowers and twinkling lights that were a feast for the senses. As she grew older, she realized there were contradictions between the two faiths. A number of youth groups spoke of Vaishnavite domination, and initiated campaigns for reclaiming ancient Sanamahi shrines.

A Vaishnavite priest, Shanti Goswami, had come from Bengal in 1704, during the reign of Medingu Charainongba, and introduced the Vaishnavite faith. Maharaja Garib Niwaz, who ascended the throne in 1713, converted to Vaishnavism. He became intolerant of Sanamahism, burned *phuyas*, ancient sacred texts, and exiled those who refused to adopt Vaishnavite Hinduism. The exiles were called 'lois', and later classified as low-caste—the Scheduled Castes of Manipur.

Sanamahism is relatively egalitarian in its value system. With the ascendance of Vaishnavism, egalitarianism took a drubbing. Ethnic, gender and class differences took on sharper contours. Pacha Loishang, an all-woman court of justice dealing with family issues, which began at the time of Leima Leisna, declined during the nineteenth century. Garib Niwaz handed over its headship to a male scion of the royal family. Women's status declined overall, and Maibis were relegated to the background.

Maibis continue, however, to hold an important place in Manipuri society, as mediums vitally in touch with supernatural forces. When Tonsija Devi told Sharmila about the Maibis of old, the young girl had no problem visualizing them, for she had seen and met a number of Maibis living near her home. She watched, enchanted, as they led the sacred Lai Haraoba dance in April each year. To this day, Maibis have many sacred duties, like healing, counselling and making prophecies.

Back in Garib Niwaz's time, people rebelled against forced conversions. His third wife, Queen Wahengbam Paikhu Panthobi, revolted against the policy, threw him into exile and placed her son on the throne of Manipur. During subsequent decades, Maharajas Bhagyachandra and Chandrakirti patronized Vaishnavism. Most Meiteis adopted elements of Vaishnavism, but did not give up their ancient faith. Subsequent generations became accustomed to following an intricate mix of the two systems.

Christian missionaries attempted to spread their faith in Manipur from the late nineteenth century onwards. They found little opening among the Meiteis, but were welcomed by a number of hill tribes. None of the ethnic communities was interested, however, in completely shedding its ancient beliefs. An attitude of careful syncretism prevailed here as well. Various hill people embraced Christianity, but never entirely discarded their older animistic faiths. They continued to honour and worship powerful ancestral spirits, and the forces of nature, even as they adopted important Christian tenets.

As Sharmila grew up, she found some young neighbours and members of her family involved in the movement for Sanamahi revivalism. The new generation of youth questioned and challenged imposed cultures, and initiated struggles to reclaim cultural roots.

ॐ

Manipur may appear isolated and self-contained, but has in fact served as a thoroughfare over the centuries. Countless travellers, missionaries, merchants and warriors, from 'mainland'

India, China and South-East Asia have traversed its valley and
hill routes. The state shares a long border with Myanmar
towards the east. Mizoram lies to its south, Assam to the west
and Nagaland to the north.

The kingdom of Manipur was known by different names
at different times, important among them being Kangleipak
and Cassay. The present name was conferred in the eighteenth
century, under the influence of Vaishnavite culture. It means,
literally, 'the land of jewels'.

The monarchical state is said to have explicitly pursued
goals of collective growth and even-handed justice—principles
usually traced to Sanamahism, which is inherently opposed to
casteism, women's subordination and degradation of human
beings.[5] A well-organized social order was considered essential
for the maintenance of cosmic equilibrium. A sophisticated
apparatus developed for administration and revenue collection.

At the same time, the infamous Lallup system developed,
and was strictly enforced: it required all men, from hills and
plains, to perform service to the state, for ten days out of
every forty. Various types of service, military and non-military,
were extracted. Because of this, men were frequently absent
from their homes.

Women learnt to manage in the absence of men, and assumed
a central role in agriculture and trade. They produced goods
within the homestead, and carried the ware to the market in
self-made wicker baskets. Khwairamband, Nambol, Thoubal,
Moirang, Moreh, Ningthoukhong, Kakching, and other local
markets came to be known as Ima markets. Women handled
the trade between hills and plains. At specified spots in the
foothills, valley traders would wait with merchandise, for
their counterparts from the hills to come down with specific

commodities and products. This system of internal trade was known as *ngai*.

Leikais, villages, functioned on the basis of mutual cooperation. Cultivators performed intensive agricultural operations in teams, a system of mutual help called *khutlang*. Cooperative farming saved labour and money for each family. Before a marriage, the groom's friends built a house or *yaongsang*, for the new couple. An ill or dying person was looked after day and night by other villagers. After death, each household contributed wood for the burial. Sharmila observed these customs, like others around, when she was growing up.

༁

During long centuries of coexistence, serious sources of conflict also existed. Spread over an area of 22,327 square kilometres, Manipur has two distinct physical regions—a flat oval-shaped valley encompassing around 2,200 square kilometres of fertile land interspersed with wetlands, and an outlying hilly area. Farming in the hills is largely subsistence based, while cultivation in the valley is reasonably productive. Political power has been concentrated with Meiteis—about 70 per cent of the state's population—who inhabit the valley, which is barely 10 per cent of the total land area. Nagas and Kuki-Chins typically inhabit the hills, which means they spread out over nearly 90 per cent of the land area. Such imbalances, and rivalries within ethnic groups, have been sources of tension.

Territorial and power conflicts erupted sporadically. During the reign of King Ninghtou Khomba (1432–67), Tangkhul

Nagas marched towards Imphal to capture Kangla and raid paddy from the state granary when the king was away. Queen Linthoingambi dressed in king's robes, and her maids dressed as soldiers, went on horseback to confront the invaders. The invading army beat a hasty retreat. They then approached the queen who, dressed in her own robes, entertained them with wine and tobacco leaves. When they grew inebriated, she had them captured. On another occasion, the same queen, again camouflaged as the king, defeated the Khongjais of Khongyang.

Sharmila learnt that by the seventeenth century, Manipur was a leading regional power. Aung San Suu Kyi records, 'In 1635, the Burmese kings moved their capital to Ava. The following century brought a tangle of trouble with the Shans, Chinese, Thais, Mons and the Indian border state of Manipur.'[6] Manipur and Burma (Myanmar) were often at war. In 1762 Maharaja Jai Singh signed a treaty with the English East India Company, for assistance to keep the Burmese at bay. In return, Manipur granted land for factories and forts, and open trade facilities. This treaty, called the Anglo-Manipuri treaty, gave the Company a foothold in Manipur.

The Manipur–Burma War raged during 1819–26, a period called the Seven Year Devastation. Manipuris still recall this period with horror. The Burmese took many prisoners of war. Imprisoned women had to pound paddy by day, and reportedly submit to forced sex with soldiers by night. Maharaja Gambhir Singh made every effort to liberate Manipur, but his army could not find a way into the heavily garrisoned camp at Kabow valley. Captured women communicated through folk songs, sung while pounding paddy, that the only way to break into the camp was to dry up the surrounding moat, by blocking the source of water. The Manipuri army did so, entered the camp and routed the Burmese.

The East India Company helped Maharaja Gambhir Singh during this war. After the war he signed the Treaty of Yandaboo, by which Manipur gave the Kabow valley to Burma. Maishna Kumudini, Gambhir Singh's chief queen, fought at his side in the Indo-Burmese war. After Gambhir Singh's death, his agent Nar Singh usurped the throne. Kumudini fled to Cachar with her son, Crown Prince Chandrakirti. When he grew up, Chandrakirti rode in with his army and reclaimed the throne of Manipur. When Kumudini returned, Chandrakirti received her with fifty-five gun salutes.

It is believed that genocide during the Indo-Burmese war reduced the population of the Imphal valley to just about 10,000 people, with substantially more women than men.[7] By the late nineteenth century, the sex ratio evened out, largely due to influx of males, including Muslims, called Pangals, and Brahmans. Many male migrants married local women, and were assimilated into Manipuri society.

Women of Manipur had, over past centuries, established a right—to collectively present grievances and demands to the king. The king was bound to give the women a respectful hearing. Sometimes he even granted reprieve to criminals sentenced to death, if women spoke up on behalf of the condemned persons[8]—a right to clemency probably unique among the peoples of the world.

Women often used their right of appeal to correct state policies. They did not hesitate to confront the monarch, for promotion of the general interest.[9] When, for instance,

Maharaja Chandrakirti, who reigned from 1834 to 1844, once ordered men to go to the jungles to trap royal elephants, women protested against the order. They argued that men were required in the villages at that time, to harvest the crops standing ripe in the fields. Due to the women's plea, the king finally agreed to postpone the Samutanba or elephant trapping, until after the harvest season.

Thus the people tried to live in peace, looking after their own welfare, protecting life and livelihood, while war and conflict raged in and around the kingdom.

ॐ

In 1891 the British established suzerainty over Manipur. Taking advantage of internal disputes, British forces entered Kangla on the night of 23 March, but the Manipuris gathered and routed the British army. The army suffered heavy casualties, and five highly placed British officers, including the political agent of Manipur, Frank Grimwood, were beheaded. The British immediately declared war. Three columns of the British army were requisitioned from Cachar, Kohima and Burma, to make an all-out attack on Manipur. The Anglo-Manipur War culminated in the decisive battle of Khongjom on 27 April 1891. Paona Braja Basi, Chongtham Mia, Yiskul Lakpa, Sengoi Sana, Yenkhoiba, Wangkhei Meiraba, Chinglem Sana and many other generals and heroes lost their lives, and the Manipuris suffered humiliating defeat. With the takeover of Manipur, the British completed their conquest of the Indian subcontinent.

The people of Manipur were not easily subdued. The regime sentenced two leaders, Senapati Bir Tikendrajit and

Thangal General, to death for conspiring against the empire. To oppose this order, six thousand women took to the streets in protest on 13 August 1891, the day scheduled for the execution. Wearing pale pink phaneks and white inaphies symbolizing mourning, these women gathered at Mapal Kangjeibung, the public grounds near Kangla, and appealed for forgiveness. Although British governors were aware of women's special right to plead for clemency, they paid no heed. The two leaders were executed at the gallows. They have been revered as hero-martyrs ever since. The British deported Angou Senapati and other senior Manipuri leaders to Kala Pani, in the Andaman Islands.

Manipur was declared a princely state under British suzerainty, and five-year-old Churachand Singh the next ruler. The British completely destroyed the royal palace at Kangla, and members of the royal family were forcibly scattered in different directions.

Earlier, people had free access to most parts of Kangla. The public frequently worshipped at the large number of shrines situated within the extensive Kangla compound. Kangla Fort was, in fact, considered the most sacred spot in Manipur. After taking over, the British debarred people from entering this place. It was closed to the public, a deliberate act demonstrating and symbolizing colonial power. The execution of beloved heroes, and the closure of Kangla, created a fertile breeding ground for seething resentment, widespread anger and rebelliousness.

GRANDMA'S TALES AND WOMEN'S WARS

By the time Irom Tonsija Devi was born, in 1903, Manipur was no longer an independent kingdom. As she grew up she learned of Manipur's defeat at the hands of the British.

When I meet Tonsija Devi in April 2007, in Imphal, she is 104 years old. I wait for an hour while she finishes her morning meal—a bowl of rice, red sugar and a banana. Resplendent in crisp white blouse and phanek, she comes out and sits regally on a rug spread out on the mud floor of the front veranda. Her voice is robust as she greets us, holds out a gnarled hand, peers at us with pale watery eyes, smiles tenderly and says, in Meiteilon, 'I feel a lot of love for them, and a lot of pity.' Her own stable life, in the lap of nature, gives her a sense of ease and grounding that she feels we lack. As travellers from far-off Delhi and friends of her long-lost granddaughter Sharmila, she treats us with affection and kindness. I am impressed by her sparkling good health, confident longevity and sheer rootedness. It is true her eyes are no longer sharp, and her mind wanders. Her son Manglem Singh tells us she gets stuck and keeps repeating phrases, so he is reluctant to put questions to her.

There is one question I insist he ask her: what does she recall of the Second Nupilan? I have realized that in 1939, when the Second Women's War was fought in Manipur, Tonsija would have been around thirty-five years old—Sharmila's current age. I'm wondering whether there is a line of influence, an invisible strain, connecting the two women, transmitting the spirit of rebellion from one generation to another.

The question brings forth a flood of vivid memories. Tonsija Devi becomes animated, articulate and coherent. She explains at once, 'The price of paddy was 25 paise for about 30 kilos. All of a sudden the price rose to 3 or 4 rupees. It became impossible for people to buy rice. Rice was sent out of Manipur, while people were starving. Women streamed in from all sides—all the women of Manipur. I was there. We spent days outside the Durbar, and finally we won. The Maharaja heard us. He ordered the price of paddy to be brought down. The price was brought down. So we could all eat, and live as before.'

She says, 'We women carried our *tem*s with us during the Nupilan.' The tem is a wooden implement used in weaving. The women used it as a weapon of defence. Manglem Singh's son, a thoughtful young man named Milan, brings out a tem for us to view. It is black, sturdy, nearly sword shaped. It seems to symbolize the lives of many women of Manipur—weaving cloth, and seeking to weave peace too, within the social fabric.

༄

Sharmila grew up listening to the stories Tonsija Devi told her about the Nupilans. Tonsija was just a year old at the time of the First Nupilan, in 1904. These 'women's wars' against imperialism are still recalled with fierce pride.

People were angry at their loss of sovereignty, compounded by an alien judicial and administrative system. Women's right of appeal, honoured over the centuries, had been revoked. Such injustice was unacceptable to ordinary people, such as Tonsija Devi's family. Her family lived in Shinzamai Bazar, near the centre of Imphal city. It was an ordinary working-class family, fervently patriotic, with strong women who actively participated in the Nupilans.

The British dismantled traditional courts of justice and replaced them with Western procedures and laws. They set up a British-style bureaucratic system, and used divide-and-rule policies which exaggerated ethnic divisions. They placed most hill regions under a separate administrative structure, based on direct central supervision. Taking advantage of ethnic feuds, they used Kukis to fight Nagas, and tried to further their own position by acting as mediators.

On 16 March 1904, the State Bungalow in the occupation of Captain Nuthall, tutor to Maharaja Churachand Singh, and of Dunlop, assistant political agent, Manipur, was burnt to the ground. In early July 1904, twenty-eight sheds housing 3,000 women vendors at Khwairamband Bazaar, Imphal, were burnt. Authorities were unable to trace the arsonists. On 4 August, the bungalow to which Captains Nuthall and Dunlop had shifted, was also burnt down. Unable to locate the culprits, Political Agent H. Maxwell issued an order in late September, imposing a collective punishment: Imphal's menfolk must go to Kabow valley, fetch teakwood, bamboo and other materials, and build new bungalows for the British officers. The public petitioned for repeal of this order, but Maxwell ignored the petition. Several local people were imprisoned on grounds of suspicion. A ban was imposed on gatherings of five or more persons.

Men began preparing to go to Kabow to put in forced labour, seeing no way out, but women refused to accept the unjust punishment. In early October, thousands of women began to gather and demonstrate on the main roads of Imphal, demanding withdrawal of the order for forced labour. Women vendors led the movement. Prominent leaders included Sanajaobi Devi, Leishangthem Kethabi, Dhaballi Devi and Laishram Ningol Jubati—all working-class women.

The British tried to quell the agitation, summoning army reinforcements from neighbouring areas. But their efforts proved unsuccessful. They put up a blockade, but protesters broke through by swimming across the river at various points. Finally, the British had to give in to popular sentiment, and withdraw the unjust order.

☙

Tonsija grew up in the thick of unrest. Women would arrive at the market by dawn, carrying baskets of vegetables and condiments, poultry and fish. They came from villages in and around Imphal city, and discussed contemporary affairs with a sharp awareness. Her mother and other women of the family were part of this large, assorted group. They wove cloth for sale, and grew vegetables in tiny kitchen gardens and sold the surplus. She absorbed this way of life—the political excitement as well as a traditional life of hard work, carried on with diligence and care.

After Tonsija married Irom Modon Singh, she moved to the Irom family settlement in Kongpal Kongkhom Leikai, at the edge of Imphal city. The ever-growing cluster of Irom homes melded seamlessly into fields and hills on the far horizon. Until 1891, men regularly served in the royal palace for part of the year. Even after British takeover, some forms of Lallup, ritual service, continued. Men also sought jobs in the city. Tonsija joined the Irom women in weaving, growing vegetables, cooking and caring. The entire family took part in paddy cultivation, the fertile land yielding two crops a year.

Affairs of state powerfully affected daily life. Nobody, not even the most ordinary citizen, could escape the impact of these matters. Churachand Singh ascended the throne when he came of age in 1907, and a Durbar was constituted with the king as president, a European officer as vice-president, and five Manipuri aristocrats as members. The British continued to control critical areas: defence, foreign affairs, communication and coinage.

People placed much hope on Maharaja Churachand, but he turned out to be little more than a puppet in British hands. He became extremely unpopular when he introduced taxes on religious observances, like *chandan senkhai*, tax on sandalwood paste which Vaishnavites use regularly. His failure to revive the traditional right of women's collective representation also upset the public.

People realized they could no longer rely on a monarch to protect their accustomed rights. To the British, Manipur was a prize colony, ripe for exploitation. It was strategically located and, during the next decades, its importance grew as a source of revenue from trade in paddy and timber.

Exploitative colonial policies gave rise to discontent, which culminated, from time to time, in a series of people's movements. During 1917–19, Kukis rebelled against forced labour recruitment. Close on the heels of the Kuki Rebellion, came the Bazaar Boycott Agitation of 1920–1, followed by the Water Tax Agitation, 1925–32, the Zaliangrong Movement, 1930–2, and the Second Nupilan, 1939–42.

The Water Tax Agitation opposed increase in water tax to Rs 2 per annum, an astronomical sum at the time; people were jailed if they failed to pay the tax. The Zaliangrong Movement was a militant struggle against Christian conversions, forced labour recruitment, and simultaneously for freedom from British rule.

In the mid-1920s, a movement in Tamenglong district mobilized people against unjust laws, forced labour, compulsory porterage and exorbitant house tax. Its leader, Jadonang, sought to unite Zemi, Laingmei, Rongmei and other Naga tribes, with the goal of establishing a Naga kingdom. Gaidinlieu, a thirteen-year-old girl of Ningkhao village, joined the movement in 1928. She took over leadership after the British executed Jadonang in 1931. British forces captured her in October 1932 in Pulomi village, and sentenced her to life imprisonment. She spent the major part of her life in prison, in the Mizo Hills and Meghalaya. Even after Indian independence in 1947, she spent her last years in exile in Nagaland.[10]

The British regime played havoc with Manipur's economy. They encouraged influx of Marwari merchants, who unscrupulously exploited the local populace, and lined their own pockets. Shrewd businessmen set up networks for wholesale trade in paddy, successfully displacing small vendors. They bought paddy from cultivators at low prices and, as per British policy, exported large quantities to Assam Rifles battalions at Kohima, Sadiya, Aizawl, Lokra, Darrang and Itanagar, and to some civilian sites in Assam. This export, coupled with hoarding, led to severe shortages in Manipur, raising the local price of paddy.

In 1939, excessive rain damaged the paddy crop, exacerbating the situation. Marwari traders bought paddy at throwaway prices, creating an artificial famine. They set up electric mills, causing women paddy-pounders to lose their livelihood. The artificially created famine triggered off a strong response from the women of Manipur. The Second Nupilan thus began, with women petitioning the British political agent for a ban on rice export. He ignored the petition, after which there was a popular uprising. The uprising carried on for nearly three years, until the Second World War and Japanese bombing of Imphal on 10 May 1942.

Thousands of ordinary women like Irom Tonsija Devi were the main protagonists of both Nupilans. Thirty-six-year-old Tonsija threw herself into the movement, joining the surging crowds of women coming in from all sides. She enjoyed her family's support, and could comfortably leave her children at home, when she stayed out for rallies and night-long vigils.

The Second Nupilan is etched in the consciousness of every Manipuri. Tonsija often recounted its events to her grandchildren, cherishing its memory even in old age. She recalled that the British and the Maharaja tried to trick the women, but failed. 'All the women of Manipur' finally prevailed!

After the authorities ignored their petition, on 11

December 1939 a women's delegation confronted the president of Manipur State Durbar, T.A. Sharpe. The delegation was headed by Chaobiton Devi. Sharpe promised to announce a ban order the next day, but he failed to do so. About a thousand women then intercepted paddy carts, which were travelling towards merchants' godowns. Capturing the carts, the women parked these in front of the Durbar. They continued to press their demand for cancellation of merchants' permits for rice export. Sharpe claimed he was helpless without orders from the king. The king, Maharaja Churachand, was away in Bengal.

The crowd of protesters kept swelling. They forced Sharpe to proceed to the telegraph office and send a telegram to the Maharaja. Surreptitiously, Sharpe summoned the 4th Assam Rifles regiment to disperse the crowd. Leaders Chaobiton Devi, Ibemhal Devi, Tongou Devi and others sat inside the telegraph office, while outside thousands stood vigil. By evening, 4,000 agitators surrounded the telegraph office. Policemen and sepoys attacked these unarmed women. The women defended themselves with stones and tems. About thirty women sustained injuries inflicted by batons, bayonets and rifle butts, and twenty-one had to be hospitalized.

On 13 December, Khwairamband Bazaar vendors called a strike to protest the previous days' violence. The same day, Political Agent C. Gimson announced he had received a telegram from the Maharaja ordering immediate ban on export of rice, except to Kohima and the 4th Assam Rifles, Imphal. The telegram directed Gimson and Sharpe to respect the wishes of the Imas. This signalled a major victory for the people.

Bands of protesters went to rice mill owners and made

them sign agreements promising to close down their mills. Next day, they ransacked a mill that was still running. On 17 December, protesters lodged a complaint with the political agent and Maharaja Churachand, demanding punishment to 4th Assam Rifles for inflicting violence on 12 December. Gimson dismissed the complaint, saying that the crowd had provoked the attack. On 28 December, the women intercepted thirteen bullock carts carrying paddy to the wholesale market.

Many sympathizers like Hijom Irabot, Kulabidhu Singh, Amuleishang Singh, Shri Bidur and Ibungohal Singh actively supported the Second Nupilan. At a rally on 7 January 1940, Irabot, leftist leader of the Praja Sammelan, lauded the bravery of Manipur's womenfolk. The British thereupon arrested Irabot, and sentenced him to three years' imprisonment. On 14 January, women protesters held a meeting in Police Lane, defying Maharaja Churachand's orders.

The Second Nupilan burgeoned into a demand for democratic government. Women leaders Rajni Devi and Wangkhem Kumari advised women to confront officials who demanded exorbitant taxes. When Sawombung forest officials tried to collect tax from local women carrying forest produce for sale in Imphal, protesters confronted the corrupt officials, even ransacking their offices. Many similar incidents took place. Each woman would arm herself with a tem and wear two phaneks, before going out to confront injustice. The authorities imprisoned several leaders, including Wahengbam ongbi Tonkhombini, Nonghtombam ongbi Khongnangne, Khetrimayum ongbi Oinam, and Thongom ongbi Amubi. The people resisted, and widespread unrest continued. Markets remained shut for as long as three years.

Gimson threatened women vendors with dire consequences if they failed to open the markets, but the women stood firm, assuring him that they would open the markets once their demands were met.

The British were badly shaken by the popular demand for democratic self-governance, which emerged out of the Second Nupilan. After World War II, the movement for democracy, led by Hijom Irabot and the Manipur Congress, continued to gain ground.

ॐ

On 11 August 1947, Maharaja Bodh Chandra of Manipur and Governor General Louise Mountbatten signed a Standstill Agreement and Instrument of Accession by which Manipur was granted dominion status. On 15 August, Manipur became a sovereign state, and the Manipuri Pakhangba-embedded Royal Flag replaced the British Union Jack at Kangla Fort. The Maharaja framed the Manipur State Constitution Act, 1947, and Manipur formulated its own Consititution. Elections were held for the Manipur State Legislative Assembly in 1948, on the basis of universal adult franchise with secret ballot. A democratic government was sworn in, with the Maharaja as its constitutional head. The Maharaja appointed a chief minister in consultation with his council of ministers.

Inexplicably, on 21 September 1949, the Maharaja signed the Manipur Merger Agreement, under which, on 15 October 1949, Manipur became a Grade C state of the Indian Union. He signed the agreement without consulting the council of ministers or the Legislative Assembly.

The people of Manipur saw this merger as a great betrayal

by the Indian government, who somehow tricked the Maharaja. After the Merger Agreement, the Government of India dissolved the democratically elected Legislative Assembly of Manipur, disbanded its council of ministers and rendered its Constitution ineffective.

These core issues remain highly controversial. Some historians hold that between 15 August 1947 and 15 October 1949, Manipur was indeed an independent state; the Indian government forced the Maharaja to sign the Merger Agreement, a step never ratified by the elected representatives of the people of Manipur. Another set of historians believes, however, that after signing the Standstill Agreement and the Instrument of Accession in 1947, Manipur was already part of the political framework of India. As such, it did not enjoy a sovereign, independent status.

When the Constitution of India was inaugurated on 26 January 1950, Manipur was included as a Part C state. Popular struggles for restoration of democratic governance peaked by the mid-1950s, and led to Manipur being upgraded to the status of a Union territory in 1956. Territorial Council elections were held in 1957. But the people's movements continued, since the Territorial Council had no legislative, judicial or financial powers. Subsequently, Manipur was upgraded to a Territorial Assembly, with legislative powers.

In 1968, the All Manipur Statehood Demand Committee was formed. It organized mass rallies, demonstrations and dharnas, with the aim of achieving full statehood. Manipur was declared a full-fledged state of the Indian Union in 1972—the year that, amid general jubilation and hope, Irom Sharmila was born in Imphal.

FLAMING TORCHES

Despite becoming a full-fledged state in 1972, life hardly improved for the common people of Manipur. They soon grew disillusioned and articulated their grievances and demands. They resisted various governmental policies, pointing out the deleterious effect on their lives.

In the 1970s Manipuri women organized themselves as a strong defensive force against the government's policy of liberally licensing liquor vends.

This policy, put into place in the early '70s and vigorously pursued thereafter, aimed at revenue generation, unmindful of the social and health effects. Scarce household resources instead of providing for food and other necessities were getting used up in alcohol. Newspapers reported cases of domestic violence, wife beating and child battering under influence of liquor; a man beat his wife to death because she refused to give him money for alcohol. Women gathered around these issues.

Many scholars remark on the prominence of women as powerful dissenting figures in Manipur. 'The ancient and medieval period of folk oral literature of Manipuri language was the literature of protest. The protagonist was always a woman ... The nucleus of female power in the group form is intact [even today].'[11]

Irom Sharmila was influenced by the tradition of collective womanpower and its continuance into the present age. During her growing years, women in different parts of the state were waging powerful anti-alcoholism struggles. This became famous as the Nisha Bandh, anti-alcoholism, movement. It made its presence felt in no uncertain terms, keeping women's human rights concerns alive in the public sphere.

All over the state, women resented the government's liquor policy, ill effects of which penetrated into their everyday lives. On 30 December 1974, a woman went to the liquor shop in Turel Awand Leikai, to fetch her husband home. The shop owner beat her up. A large group of women, incensed by this act, gathered at the shop and protested the beating. They held a meeting and resolved to campaign against the alcohol policy, forming an organization—the first Nisha Bandh or anti-alcoholism group. Kshetrimayum Achoubi Devi, a schoolteacher, was elected its president, and N. Modhu Singh, an advocate, its secretary.

Over the next few months, the Nisha Bandh movement took shape in several parts of the state. Women formed local Nisha Bandh chapters, and moved around in groups, to apprehend drunkards. Walking about at night, they carried torches or lanterns, caught drunken persons, and imposed fines on them. They raided liquor vends and set fire to alcohol supplies. Because they moved around at night carrying flaming torches, many people informally called them 'Meira Paibis', women who carry flaming torches.

Women also mobilized against unrestrained trade in drugs. Addiction to heroin, morphine and pethidine, and pharmaceutical drugs like Mandrax, was becoming rampant.

Numerous jungle routes, particularly along the Manipur–Myanmar border, were being utilized by drug traffickers.

The activists soon realized more could be achieved if they consolidated local struggles. Nisha Bandh groups met together on 21 April 1976, to discuss the need for joint action. They passed a resolution demanding a statewide ban on liquor and drugs. The groups formed a state-level organization called All Manipur Women's Social Reformation and Development Samaj (AMWSRDS). Its first president was Chaobi Devi, and its first secretary, Momon Devi. However, the problems remained intractable. A few years later—on 4 April 1980—an All-Manipur Bandh was organized, to push for a ban on liquor and drugs.

Nisha Bandhis made a significant impact. Apart from tackling drug addiction and alcoholism, the movement raised issues of inheritance rights, price rise, dowry demands, domestic violence and sexual abuse. They took up these issues in right earnest, and set up local shelters for survivors of domestic violence.

ᢗ

From 1980 onwards, Nisha Bandh groups increasingly took up issues related to militarization and military excesses. At this point, they gave up the term Nisha Bandhi, and began identifying themselves simply as Meira Paibis. Whereas the name Nisha Bandhis indicated their earlier preoccupation with anti-alcoholism, the new term was more inclusive, signifying a broader range of core concerns.

By this time, insurgency had proliferated in the state. Right from 1949, there was public discontent over what many viewed as a forced merger with the Indian Union. A handful of rebels refused to cooperate with the Union, raising the demand for independence. Chronic neglect of Manipur, by the Centre, drew more supporters to the insurgents' side. From a small number of rebellious young men, the ranks of the insurgents grew significantly.

The state sent in security forces, with a mandate to capture insurgents. Reports trickled in of security personnel picking up youngsters at random, arresting, harassing and torturing them. Initially, many Nisha Bandhis believed the arrests were justified. They themselves disagreed with insurgents' methods and tried to prevent young men from joining the insurgent groups. But soon they came to realize that many innocent young men, who had no links with insurgency, were being picked up by the security forces.[12]

The activist women began focusing on the issue of state atrocities on youngsters. A particular case is recalled as a turning point, demonstrating their shift in focus, from anti-alcoholism to the struggle against state atrocities. This case concerned inhumanities committed in Langjing village. On 26 April 1980, two Central Reserve Police Force (CRPF) personnel died in a bomb blast. The blast was set off by unknown insurgents, whom the CRPF was unable to track down. In retaliation, CRPF personnel carried out a combing operation in Langjing village and arrested many innocent people. They reportedly tortured men and raped women. The casualty department at the nearby hospital became packed with wounded villagers. When women of Chingamakha, Imphal, heard about the atrocities, they immediately went to Langjing, and investigated the situation. They spoke out against the arrest, torture and rape of innocent people. The women appealed to insurgent groups to stop carrying out ambushes, particularly near villages, since security forces subsequently tortured innocent villagers. After this particular case, the Nisha Bandhi became popularly known as Meira Paibis.

A day after the Langjing carnage, a CRPF jawan killed a woman at Khwairamband Bazaar and seriously injured another person. The Government of Manipur issued curfew orders in Imphal. When Khwairamband Bazaar reopened on 9 May 1980, women traders demanded removal of the CRPF from the bazaar area.

Instead, Chief Minister Dorendro Singh announced that due to the deteriorating law and order situation, he was handing over administration of the state to the Indian army. Almost the entire state of Manipur was declared a Disturbed Area, and stiff counter-insurgency measures enacted. The major measure amongst these was the AFSPA—a draconian emergency law—ostensibly to help curb insurgency.

$$\mathcal{T}$$

The public, led by women, challenged the imposition of army rule. On 14 May 1980, thousands of women submitted a memorandum to the chief minister demanding removal of the Disturbed Area clause, and revocation of AFSPA. They held a mass meeting at Mapal Kangjeibung in Imphal, and resolved unanimously to form an organization called Manipur Nupi Kanglup (MNK), to keep up the momentum. MNK organized a rally on 28 May, at which some 10,000 women gathered, defying a ban on mass meetings. The police cracked down on the gathering.

A large number of women were arrested, bundled into a truck and taken to Pangei, at the outskirts of Imphal. En route, a twenty-five-year-old pregnant woman, Piyari Devi of Salanthong, fell down from the overcrowded truck. She died on the spot. Ima Taruni, a senior Meira Paibi, relates, 'The government did not care. But we could not bear the loss of one precious life. After Piyari's death, we became all the more committed to the cause of putting an end to all such atrocities.'[13] Meira Paibis pressurized the government to conduct a judicial enquiry into Piyari's death. Later—in 1999—Manipuri activists and intellectuals decided to celebrate 28 May every year, as Meira Paibi Day. In 1999, Meira Paibi Day was observed in Gandhi Memorial Hall, Imphal, with Ima Mangol Devi, a senior Meira Paibi leader, as chairperson.

On 8 September 1980, the entire state was declared a Disturbed Area. On 29 December 1980, insurgents planted three bombs near Tomal Makhong. J&K Rifles launched a combing operation, and arrested an innocent youngster called Ibomcha, who was sleeping on the veranda of his home in Liwa Lambi Maibam Leikai. Local Meira Paibis went to the J&K Rifles camp and requested that Ibomcha be released. In response, the forces actually handed over Ibomcha to his family that very evening. This was a resounding victory for women's collective strength. From that day on, whenever the army came to pick up a youngster, Meira Paibis demanded to know why, and tried to save the young person. Every year, 29 December is observed as Pari Kanba Numit—the day to save and protect the sons.

Seeking to root out the problem of state atrocities, Meira Paibis demanded withdrawal of AFSPA. They argued that unless the Act is removed, youngsters would continue to join underground groups. Rather than curb insurgency, the Act is actually motivating young people to become insurgents.

Ima Taruni notes[14] that sometimes Meira Paibis are wrongly labelled 'mothers of insurgents'. It is true that insurgents are after all sons and daughters of vegetable vendors, fisher folk and other ordinary people. They are fundamentally a part of society. Lacking good education, job opportunities and dignified livelihood options, a number of youngsters, frustrated and angry, take up arms. That is why elderly women sometimes say that both insurgents and innocent boys are like their own sons. Meira Paibis consistently try to protect youngsters from the recruitment efforts of insurgent groups.

All over the state, women set up Meira Paibi groups in their localities. Ordinary women of villages and towns formed the rank and leadership of these groups. Meira Paibis patrolled neighbourhoods at night, flaming torches held aloft, to safeguard their communities against search operations by security forces. When something untoward happened, anybody could sound an alarm by banging a stone against a lamp post. Hearing this, activist women would rush to the spot. Meira Paibi groups from neighbouring areas were summoned whenever extra support was required. Meira Paibis set up shelters, called Meira Shanglens, in their localities. As insurgency grew and 'counter-insurgency' intensified, the Meira Paibis became increasingly vigilant.

☙

Valleyrose Hungyo, editor of Tangkhul newspaper *Aja Daily*, recalls that in 1967, when she was just ten, the army attacked her village. A number of villagers were displaced, never to return; many were killed. The government provided no records of villages destroyed in the name of counter-insurgency. In 1974, a young Tangkhul girl in the same village was raped, and she later committed suicide. The community, especially women, rose in protest and formed the Tangkhul Shanao Long.[15]

Over the years, virtually every community in Manipur developed a strong women's front, like the Tangkhul Shanao Long. These include the Naga Mother's Association, Kuki Women's Association, Lamkang Women's Union, Mayan Women's Union and Chothe Women's Union. These groups became well known as active guardians of their communities, and campaigners for women's rights. In 1994, women from thirteen Naga tribes of Manipur met in Ukhrul and formed the Naga Women's Union, to campaign for women's rights, and strive for peace through women's mediation.

In 1975, students from Kohima formed the Naga People's Movement for Human Rights (NPMHR). Subsequently, concerned citizens formed similar organizations in different parts of Manipur. In 1993, Nagas from Nagaland and Manipur came together in Kohima and formed an umbrella organization, in defence of human rights.

Women's organizations consistently drew attention to the deteriorating condition of women in families and society. Bonds with sisters were once highly valued, crystallizing in festivals like *ningol chaukoba*, in which brothers invited married sisters and plied them with gifts and food. But today, a widowed woman is likely to be insulted and thrown out by her in-laws as well as by her own brothers, particularly if she tries to discuss inheritance of parental property. Brothers induce sisters to sign away inherited land or property. Bureaucratic tangles also render it difficult for women to keep control over their property.[16]

Professor Yamini Devi, who heads the newly formed Manipur State Commission for Women, notes a steep rise in crimes of abduction and forced elopement. High dowry demands have become routine in a society that until recently practised bride price. Suicides by young women are increasing. Trafficking of girls and women, rape and sexual harassment are on the rise. Women are prey to overwork, chronic exhaustion, physical collapse and mental and emotional breakdown.[17] They look after the health of the whole family, but nobody attends to their health. They survive only because they maintain healthy habits and traditional cooking practices, with plenty of green vegetables and fish. Remarkably, Manipur has one of the lowest rates of anaemia in the country, among girls and women. The credit goes to the genius of the Manipuri women, who have mastered strategies to cope with harsh conditions.

The sex ratio in Manipur has declined from 1,015 (females per 1000 males) in 1961, to as low as 978 in 2001. The sex ratio is lowest in conflict-ridden areas, for example, just 884 in Ukhrul district (in 1991). Women's vulnerability is associated with poverty, loss of livelihood, overwork, violence, hardships due to drug abuse and alcoholism, and diseases including HIV/AIDS. In 2008, Manipur had the highest figure for HIV/AIDS relative to population, as compared with any other Indian state.

Women bear the burden of social stigma. A woman may

contract HIV from her husband, yet be labelled a loose woman, and abandoned by her in-laws.[18] Social norms or *chatnabi* impose silence upon women. Chunkham Sheelaramani, a feminist scholar, laments, 'It is a heart-breaking scene that the women of Manipur are used to abuses thrown upon them, and that they "exist" and they "survive".'[19]

The Meira Paibi movement articulates collective resistance to all forms of violence—whether committed by the state or insurgents. Meira Paibis focus increasingly on issues of state violence. At the same time they continue to pose a challenge to regressive social norms. Through their analysis and actions, they have exposed the close links existing between seemingly disparate issues: domestic violence and state violence, rape and militarization.

Meira Paibis advise the state to handle insurgents carefully, to treat them as misguided youth rather than as criminals, and to listen to their grievances. If a person is suspected to be a member of an insurgent group, proper judicial procedure should be followed to establish guilt and mete out punishment. Instead, such procedure is usually ignored and both innocent and guilty are subjected to relentless torture.[20]

INSURGENCY

Throughout her growing years, Sharmila was well aware of insurgency, a powerful force rearing its head in the society and politics of Manipur. Insurgents articulated the popular demand for dignity and 'development', but the means they chose were often violent. From an early age, Sharmila puzzled over this disconnect: how could violent means bring about peaceful ends? She developed an interest in understanding the basic sources of insurgency, but continued to disagree with the methods they used.

Right from 1949, the widespread perception that the Indian state had forced a merger upon Manipur, was a moving factor of insurgency. People not only felt that they had been tricked into joining the Indian Union, but also, thereafter, neglected and discriminated against. In 1963, the Naga Hills district of Assam was made into a separate state, but Manipur continued to be a mere Union territory for another ten years. Manipuri or Meiteilon, the ancient language written and spoken by Meiteis, the majority group of Manipur, was not included in the Eighth Schedule for years.

As democratic voices failed to influence the Centre and lead to people-oriented development, Manipuri youth grew increasingly frustrated. Already feeling cheated of sovereignty, denial of basic development was like rubbing salt on open wounds. Gross neglect and mis-governance provided fertile ground for the rise of insurgency.

Rather than respond at the incipient stages, when demands were articulated peacefully, the state routinely ignored popular protests. When their voices fell on deaf ears, people began using violence to assert themselves. This forced the government to react. The use of violence was actually fostered by government apathy.

र

One of the earliest insurgent or underground groups in the North-East was called the Federal Government of Nagaland (FGN). FGN spread its tentacles to Naga-inhabited hill districts of Manipur by 1956. It established a base in Ukhrul, and operations spilled over into the thickly forested districts of Senapati and Tamenglong. These places also became the site for insurgency operations by Nationalist Socialist Council of Nagaland (NSCN). NSCN split in 1988, to form NSCN (K) and NSCN (IM).

Arambam Somarendra set up the United National Liberation Front (UNLF) in 1964. In 1977, R.K. Tulachandra established the People's Revolutionary Party of Kangleipak (PREPAK), and in 1978, N. Biseswar raised the People's Liberation Army (PLA). UNLF was initially founded as a social organization, and aimed to consolidate the demand for independence. Its leader Rajkumar Meghen, grandson of the hero-martyr Bir Tikendrajit, was widely perceived to be a high-minded patriot.

PLA attracted a cross-section of educated youth to its fiercely leftist ideology. PREPAK and PLA conducted a series of daring ambushes and dacoities in 1978–9, snatching arms from police and security forces, and grabbing money to buy more arms.

PLA and UNLF had hideouts in Meitei villages in the valley, and camps for training cadre in Chandel district as well as Myanmar. Chandel and Churachandpur districts served as sanctuaries for PLA, PREPAK, UNLF and a host of smaller groups.

In the early 1980s the Indian army captured PLA chief Biseswar and killed a number of top leaders, halting PLA in its tracks. Biseswar took to electoral politics after his release and became an MLA, but was killed by the hardcore unit of PLA. PLA regrouped, and received training from the Kachin Independent Army in Myanmar. Around this time, due to the break-up of the Khmer Rouge in Cambodia, American and Russian arms were released in enormous numbers in the South-East Asian clandestine arms market. Virtually all insurgent groups tried to build up their arsenal by buying arms, available in Myanmar in large quantities, across the border at Chandel.

FGN introduced extortion in Manipur, and NSCN (IM) systemized it into annual house tax, ration tax, taxes on buses, trucks and contractors. UNLF and PLA initially took donations for social activities, but this gradually transformed into extortions, which became institutionalized by the '90s. All those earning an income—businessmen, politicians, bureaucrats, doctors, lawyers and other professionals—were made to pay systematic taxes to insurgent groups. The insurgents took to siphoning off rice, petrol, diesel and kerosene oil from the public distribution system. Politicians and bureaucrats had already set the trend of siphoning off goods, and development funds. Insurgent groups, which initially opposed such corruption, began to help themselves to a major share in the graft.

❦

There is a bewildering array of underground groups in Manipur today, including over thirty banned insurgent organizations such as UNLF, PREPAK, PLA, Revolutionary People's Front (RPF), Kangleipak Communist Party (KCP), Kanglei Yagol Kanna Lup (KYKL), NSCN (IM), NSCN (K), Kuki National Organization (KNO), Kuki National Army (KNA), Kuki Liberation Organization (KLO), Kuki Liberation Army (KLA), Zoumi Revolutionary Army (ZRA) and Hmar People's Convention/Democratic (HPC/D).

UNLF remains one of the oldest and most prominent underground groups. The UNLF manifesto clearly voices a demand for self-determination, proposing plebiscite so that people can decide the future status of Manipur. Over time, UNLF has become more flexible: they no longer oppose elections, rather talk of fundamental change *within* the existing system, and are ready to negotiate with the government.

An erstwhile UNLF leader, K. Oken, formed KYKL in 1990, after walking out of UNLF; he teamed up with splinter groups of PREPAK and KCP. KYKL tries to bring about reforms to help people in their daily lives. It started 'Operation New Kangleipak', under which anybody convicted of using unfair means in education is issued a warning; if he persists, he is severely punished, even perhaps sentenced to death. The KNO and KNA were set up in 1992–3. Later a group broke off from KNO and formed the KLO and KLA.

Insurgent groups have diverse aspirations. Most Naga groups support the demand for Greater Nagaland or Nagalim. This is bitterly opposed by UNLF and several other groups, since it would mean relinquishing nearly 40 per cent of Manipur's territory. Most Kuki groups demand a Zelengam or Kukiland.

There has been infighting between underground groups and a number of violent clashes between different ethnic communities, particularly since the 1990s. Naga–Kuki, Kuki–Aomi, Kuki–Paite, Meitei–Pangal and Meitei–Naga clashes have erupted, leading to bloodshed, displacement and severe disruption of normal life. Underlying ethnic enmity is a bitter struggle for land and resources, whose value is appreciating with the introduction of capitalist relations.

A number of underground groups support candidates from different political parties. Guided by a mix of ideology and opportunism, many have stooped to openly rigging elections, or using arms to get their way. The increasing hold of these groups upon Manipuri politics and economy is reflected in forced extortions, frequent blockades and bandhs, exacerbated inter-ethnic tensions and escalating perceptions of mutual threat.

ॐ

Neither the state nor the insurgents have showed much sensitivity to the sufferings of ordinary people. Underground groups resort to violence against the state, and nurture feuds amongst themselves, with innocent citizens ending up as the worst sufferers. The state is wreaking violence not only on insurgents but also on non-combatant citizens, whom it claims to protect. People suffer atrocities unleashed by the mighty Indian state as well as by relatively tiny insurgent groups.

Over the decades the insurgent groups have grown in number and intensity. Today all such groups are armed with their own militia. The machinery of violence at their command has grown increasingly sophisticated. Most of this armed machinery is directed against the state.

Popular perception is ambivalent in its attitudes towards insurgents. Ordinary people, struggling to make ends meet, partly see insurgents as zealous warriors putting their lives on the line to ensure that right prevails over wrong. Some insurgent groups have helped poor villagers, peasants and labourers. For instance PLA and UNLF would siphon off resources from the public distribution system, and sell the rice and kerosene at low prices to interior villages in Chandel and Churachandpur districts, thus earning for themselves a Robin Hood image. Especially in remote parts of the state, insurgent groups initially mushroomed partly because of an underlying sense of sympathy among ordinary people.

Yet, this sympathy has been on the wane, with underground groups adopting increasingly violent methods, and turning upon common people rather than protecting them. They have deliberately created a fear psychosis in order to extort money, force people to provide shelter and food, and pressurize youth to join them. The Robin Hood image is no longer dominant. Instead, insurgents are feared and hated.

As an editorial in the *Sangai Express* (October 2008) puts it:

Manipur is today on the map of terrorism and we can no longer afford to pretend otherwise by cloaking acts of terror with some more 'acceptable' form of violence such as insurgency or militancy or extremism. Apart from the blatant acts of terrorism such as targeting the public by exploding bombs in crowded places, terrorism can also come under different modes such as firing at the house of a government official or a businessman for monetary demands. Abducting and kidnapping for ransom and at times finishing off the captive, even when the ransom demand has been met, will certainly come under acts of terrorism. Violence sponsored by the State is another instance of terrorism and the past incidents like the RIMS massacre, Heirangoithong killings, Malom massacre etc. have all been contributory factors for the present chaos and anarchy that we see all around. On the other hand, the Malom massacre gave birth to Irom Sharmila Chanu, who has today come to epitomize what determination and dedication to one's belief and conviction is all about. It is time to come to terms with this harsh reality, for the fact stands that today, people no longer feel as safe as earlier about venturing out for the day's marketing or shopping or even taking a relaxing walk during times of festivals. All terror groups come up with some fantastic ideas to justify their action.

And yet, lack of education and employment, and rampant corruption continues to attract youthful energy to insurgent groups. Many young people perceive it as the only way they can contribute to solving chronic problems that plague Manipur. Atrocities by the armed forces have the unintended effect of providing ready recruits for the underground groups.

AFSPA, THE UNLAWFUL LAW

Irom Sharmila points out that strong army presence in Manipur has intensified the trauma of common people. Ordinary citizens are trapped in a no-win situation: a cycle of deprivation and violence, with no end or resolution in sight. The rights of ordinary people are being violated daily, not only by insurgents, but also by the state in the name of 'counter-insurgency'.

Irom Sharmila's protest zeroes in upon AFSPA, the draconian law which is the core of official strategy to stem insurgency. The counter-insurgency policy in Manipur is one of suppression, rather than negotiation. The thrust is anti-people, in the garb of democratic polity. Genuine public grievances are not addressed, instead there is overwhelming reliance on repressive legal and military measures.

These measures continue despite the fact that they have not had the expected results. Counter-insurgency is clearly helping to further fuel insurgency, rather than contain it. Wherever insurgents are captured or killed, more come up; whenever innocents are captured or killed by security forces, people's anger flares up, breeding more insurgents. The number of underground groups and their cadre has been continually multiplying, even as state measures to control them have intensified.

Militarization, in the name of counter-insurgency, cannot create conditions for peaceful resolution of conflicts. Yet, the official line continues to treat insurgency as a law and order problem, justifying and intensifying military 'solutions'. To be effective, counter-insurgency should in fact trace the root causes of insurgency. This requires sustained analysis by social scientists, administrators, journalists and activists, who are conversant with the area and have an ear to the ground. A detailed blueprint should be drawn up, based on this analysis. Perceived historical injustices should be directly examined, and ways toward resolution and reconciliation carefully designed.

Good governance needs to be instituted in the state. Corrupt and manipulative governance is a major factor contributing to escalation of insurgent violence. Officers at the highest levels must be accessible and accountable. If people at large find the government sincere and transparent, they would offer unconditional support to end insurgency.

From time to time, the government has devised measures to win over the population, like 'Operation Sadbhavna' under which the army supports small-scale developmental projects in remote parts of the North-East. These measures are a step in the right direction, but insufficient to meet the situation. The basic thrust of 'counter-insurgency' remains unchanged: the use of coercive methods, rather than a realistic treatment of insurgents as citizens, whose demands require political solution.

Most citizens today perceive the armed forces as little different from an army of occupation. Official reports speak of 'warfare', implicitly suggesting that the army is at war in the North-East, pitted against its own citizens.

<u>Annual Report—Army in North East—2006</u>

... During the year, continued efforts were made to modernize and upgrade weapons and weapon systems of the Army to prepare it to address the requirements of modern day warfare and enhance its combat capability.

... <u>Manipur:</u>

Sustained operations have been conducted in the three Southern districts of Manipur. The insurgents have suffered heavy attrition and huge quantity of arms and ammunition have been recovered from these areas.

The blocking of National Highway (NH)-39 by agitating Naga Student Unions of Manipur was, to some extent, offset by opening National Highway (NH)-53, as an alternate route to Imphal. Operations were conducted on a war footing on National Highway (NH)-53 and the highway was opened for traffic ...

—'Annual Report, Army in the North-east', Press Information Bureau[21]

E.N. Rammohan, ex-superintendent of police in the North-East, acknowledges that in Manipur, armed forces have committed excesses on innocents.[22] The state has witnessed a lot of corruption in counter-insurgency operations, for instance, commandos actually extract a share of the extortions made by insurgents.

He writes that transparency and accountability are essential, if counter-insurgency is to be effective. Security forces deployed should be scrupulously legal. Upright civilian, police and judicial officials should be carefully identified, and posted at crucial points in the counter-insurgency grid. They should be trained to understand specific local situations. People's lives, culture and traditions, should be respected—and never disturbed.

At present much of the force deployed in Manipur are outsiders on 'hardship postings', unable to even pronounce the names of places and peoples, and with little inclination to learn. They are ill-fitted to track down or identify insurgents, who invariably have hideouts in remote spots. Since security forces are under immense pressure to capture insurgents, they often arrest and torture the wrong people, in staged encounters. Security forces ought to hand over suspects to the police, there should be joint interrogation centres and special courts; all trials should be closely monitored. These basic democratic measures are routinely ignored.

The state should never prop up one group against another; it has done so in Manipur and other parts of the North-East. Such methods have contributed to uncontrolled escalation of violence. Counter-insurgency operations should have ensured that no unlicensed arms remain with anybody. Instead, various groups have covertly been helped to obtain arms, in order to engage in combat with other groups.

ॐ

AFSPA was introduced in some parts of Manipur in 1960, and across the entire state (except for Imphal municipality area) by 1980. Under AFSPA, military and paramilitary personnel are empowered to shoot, even kill, anybody, on grounds of mere suspicion. The Act confers impunity on security personnel: no action can be taken against them except with prior permission from the Central government.

AFSPA is a colonial legacy. The British Raj framed the Armed Force (Special Powers) Ordinance, 1942, and promulgated it on 15 August 1942 over the whole of India to quell the Quit India movement. A measure to crush the movement for Indian independence, the ordinance granted special powers to commissioned officers of the rank of captain and above to issue, in writing, shoot-to-kill order to soldiers under their command if, in their opinion, the situation so required. Manipur, being a princely state, did not come under the purview of the ordinance.

In 1955, in independent India the state of Assam passed an even more sweeping law termed the Assam Disturbed Areas Act. Under this, shoot-to-kill powers were granted to ordinary soldiers just above the rank of sepoy. While the 1942 Act stipulated that the order be written, the Assam Disturbed Area Act of 1955 had no such requirement.

In 1958, Indian Parliament passed AFSPA, ostensibly to maintain 'internal security'. In six sections, this law uses similar wording as the 1955 Act passed by the Assam legislature. AFSPA was enacted in Nagaland, to 'deal with' the Naga struggle for independence. Home Minister G.B. Pant promised it would be a temporary measure, for short and swift application. Professor N. Sanajaoba, dean of Law Faculty, Guwahati University, notes: 'Parliament did not fully apply its mind to the passage of the statute in 1958. The law, which took on emergency status, was enacted without formal declaration of emergency.'[23] In 1990, the Indian Parliament passed the Armed Forces (Jammu and Kashmir) Special Powers Act extending these repressive powers to the state of Jammu and Kashmir.[24]

In subsequent years, AFSPA was promulgated across large tracts throughout the North-East. Central and state governments progressively declared different parts of Manipur disturbed areas, imposing Disturbed Areas Act, 1976, National Security Act, 1980, and Armed Forces (Special Powers) Act, 1958. AFSPA automatically comes into force when the Union government designates a territory as a 'Disturbed Area'.

Though the entire state of Manipur was declared 'disturbed' and brought under this Act in 1980, it is still not clear what criteria are used to declare an area 'disturbed'. This is left vague.

Under this law, security forces have been granted powers for internal security management on par with defence against external aggression. This means that security forces are actually fighting a low-intensity war against what the state perceives to be 'anti-national elements'.

Government and army explain that in times of armed conflict, there is no time to wait for orders, especially if security forces are under attack. They claim that AFSPA protects soldiers against false civil and human rights cases. They prefer to overlook and ignore what is obvious: extraordinary powers, granted to armed forces personnel in a terrain most of them feel to be alien, have led to abuses and atrocities.

The Act is unambiguous about granting sweeping powers to armed forces personnel. Powers conferred under AFSPA include, under Section 4:

Any commissioned officer, non-commissioned officer or any other person of equivalent rank may, in a disturbed area, ... if he is of the opinion that it is necessary to do so for the maintenance of public order, after giving such due warning as he may consider necessary, fire upon or otherwise use force even to the causing of death, against any person who is acting in contravention of any law and order for the time being in force in the disturbed area ...

The armed forces can 'arrest, without warrant, any person who has committed a cognizable offence or against whom a reasonable suspicion exists that he has committed or is about to commit a cognizable offence, and may use such force as may be necessary to effect the arrest'. The Act empowers the personnel to search any place without warrant, even destroying it, on suspicion that it is being used by armed groups. The power to take action, earlier given to officers of the rank of captain and above, is now delegated to junior commissioned officers and non-commissioned officers. The armed forces are supposed to hand over any person they arrest to the nearest police station with the least possible delay, along with a report of the circumstances under which the arrest was made. No prosecution or other legal proceeding can be instituted against personnel acting in exercise of powers conferred by the Act, except by previous sanction of the Central government.

While the Act is meant to be deployed for short terms, in fact it has been applied continuously for decades. There is provision for a six-monthly review, but this review is carried out cursorily, or not at all.

In many ways this is an 'unlawful law'. It suspends people's fundamental rights, contravening the forty-fourth amendment to the Indian Constitution. Rule of law, democracy and judicial review are basic features of the Constitution, and cannot rightly be ignored by 'special' laws. The Act permits firing and causing death based on the slightest suspicion of an offence, which amounts to extrajudicial execution. This goes against the spirit of Article 21 of the Constitution, which promises: 'No person shall be deprived of his life or personal liberty except according to procedure established by law.' According to Justice Fazal Ali, 'procedure established by law' suggests 'certain principles of justice which inhere in every civilized system of law'.[25] It cannot be taken to allow barbaric and arbitrary use of procedure. The procedure established must be 'right and just and fair', not 'fanciful or oppressive otherwise ... Article 21 would not be satisfied. In this perspective, Section 4 of AFSPA is in fact unconstitutional, since it authorizes armed forces officers to form an "opinion" about when to fire or otherwise use force, even to the extent of causing death ...' In depriving citizens of the right to life and liberty, AFSPA is comparable to the Nuremburg laws of 1936, which allowed for extermination of Jews by the Third Reich: 'Like the Third Reich, the Indian parliament acted *intra vires* the Constitution by opening the way for killing through "procedure established by the law".'

General and customary international laws followed by the comity of nations, of which India is an inseparable part, do not countenance such suspension of fundamental rights. International humanitarian law stipulates universal standards. The protection of life, liberty and property of civilians is non-derogable under the Geneva Conventions of 1949 and 1960. Insurgents and national liberation movements are admitted into international humanitarian law, and bound by the same standards.

India is a signatory to the International Covenant on Civil

and Political Rights. Section 4 of AFSPA gives armed forces the power to kill, and is incompatible with articles 6, 9 and 14 of the Covenant. The Covenant provides that 'any person whose rights or freedoms are violated shall have an effective remedy, determined by competent judicial, administrative or legislative authorities'—a provision completely disregarded by AFSPA. Thus AFSPA is clearly incompatible with international humanitarian law.[26]

The consequences of an Act like AFSPA are a matter of grave concern. If power corrupts, absolute power has the potential to corrupt absolutely. It is hardly surprising that there has been a flood of fake encounter killings, arbitrary and summary executions, ransacking of homes, capture of innocents, and enforced disappearances. In 1997, the Supreme Court laid down guidelines regarding AFSPA, but these are frequently violated. For instance, a lady police officer is rarely present during the arrest of a woman suspect.

౭

In October 2000, while interning with Human Rights Alert in Imphal, Irom Sharmila learnt the detailed history of AFSPA. She accompanied the Independent People's Inquiry Commission to hear testimonies of victims. As she listened to experiences of innocent villagers, she came face to face with tragic, brutal violence. She felt the helplessness, despair and rage of those raped or tortured by the uniformed men, sent ostensibly to protect them.

She read whatever she could find on AFSPA and its impact on the ordinary citizens of Manipur. Asian Human Rights Commission (AHRC), Committee on Human Rights (CHR),

HRA, social workers, researchers, academics and the media jointly compiled facts regarding AFSPA in Manipur, including the excesses committed.[27] A list of violations, which is by no means exhaustive, includes details of fourteen massacres, killing over 100 persons (1980–2000); fifty-seven instances of extrajudicial execution of individuals (1980–2005); torture of eighty-three persons (1994–2004); ten cases of rape (1974–2004); and eighteen cases of enforced disappearance (1980–2000). In all these cases, AFSPA provided protection to the perpetrators.

There have been countless other atrocities, and precious little remedial action taken against the culprits, or justice of any variety whatsoever ensured. In the majority of cases, there is no documentation at all—no reports, publicity or investigation. The crimes remain buried on the spot where they occurred. For years, ordinary people of Manipur have been dwelling in a state of limbo, with their movements hemmed in by the dictat of underground groups on the one hand, and security forces on the other.

Like most ordinary people, Irom Sharmila felt helpless and desperate. She read about terrible atrocities, such as the rape of Ms Rose of Ngaprum Khullen, Ukhrul, by 95th Border Security Force (BSF) on 4 March 1974, and of Ms Luingamla, Ngaimu village, Ukhrul, by the Indian army on 24 January 1986; enforced disappearance of Mr Kangujam Loken of Khongman Makha, by 15th J&K Rifles on 23 September 1980, and of Mr Mohammed Tayab Ali of Keirang, Imphal East, by 17th Assam Rifles on 25 July 1999. She read of the extrajudicial execution of Mr Salam Somorendo of Haobam Marak, by the Indian army on 21 November 1989; torture of Mr Rangteidung of Yangkhullen village, Senapati district, by

3rd Assam Rifles on 18 August 1994; the massacre at Oinam Leikai, in which four persons were killed by the Indian army on 21 November 1980; and the Tonsen Lamkhai massacre, in which ten persons were killed by CRPF personnel on 3 September 2000.[28]

And then, on 2 November 2000, she heard of the massacre at Malom, in which ten innocent persons lost their lives.

Irom Sharmila knew she must speak up against excesses such as these. She thought deeply about what she must do. With an inner strength she had been stoking over the years, she took the unilateral decision to sit on fast. She took a clear, one-point stand: the repeal of AFSPA. To her mind, the flood of violence in Manipur would begin to abate once this undemocratic Act was withdrawn.

Irom Sharmila took up her protest, realizing she could not stay silent any longer. The Malom massacre, like the proverbial straw that broke the camel's back, broke Sharmila's silence. It is the same silence most of us adopt when up against something enormous, so enormous we do not quite know how to react. When we finally speak, the words carry power, the power built up over long years of silent endurance.

Thus quietly, from the depths of a calm ocean, a strong wave began to swell. Gathering power, it burst forth one day, taking the world by storm.

'HABITUAL OFFENDER'

'**I**will continue my fast until the Armed Forces Special Powers Act is removed. What will happen to me?—It does not matter. It is not important. I am only doing my bounden duty ...'

Sharmila's fast had an electrifying effect upon the people and politicians of Manipur. People found a voice representing their own desire for peace. The government realized it could no longer turn a blind eye and a deaf ear to people's aspirations and demands. She became a point around which dissent crystallized.

Apunba Lup, a network of thirty-two civil society organizations, had agitated against AFSPA for years. Meira Paibis, dotted across the length and breadth of Manipur, consistently spoke out against excesses committed by armed forces. Ordinary citizens felt vulnerable in an environment ruled by guns. On the one side were insurgents—often young, dissatisfied youngsters attempting revolution—and on the other were security forces, wreaking violent retribution upon a hapless population. The state of Manipur slid into a morass, its people bewildered and upset. Sharmila's protest won instant, widespread support.

Meira Paibi activists including veteran leaders Mangol Devi, popularly called Ima Mangol, and Taruni Devi, known as Ima

Taruni, joined Sharmila at Malom. The media reported her hunger strike, and the government grew alarmed. The Nambol Police arrested Sharmila, registering a First Information Report (FIR), accusing her of 'Attempt to Suicide'. This is a crime, for which a person can be sentenced up to one year of imprisonment, under Section 309 of the Indian Penal Code (IPC).

Thus began an unending saga marked by a maze of paperwork, arrests, cases, appeals, releases and rearrests, over the next few years. It is a fascinating story of quiet, firm determination expressed by the frail protester, and open confusion and concealed brutality exhibited by state power. The solidarity of people in Manipur, the rest of India and indeed many parts of the world has made it impossible for politicians to ignore her.

After arresting her, the government tried to get her to eat. She refused. A stalemate ensued. Her family and colleagues were ambivalent, since they did not want to weaken her stand, but they were not prepared to see her die either. It was a conundrum, with no black and white to it, or precise right and wrong. In a strange but understandable paradox, they agreed with police and government on one score: they wanted some physical nourishment to reach Sharmila.

As she lay in custody, her physical energy low, colleagues and family members conferred. Without nourishment, her life energy had begun to ebb. She was strict about her pledge—no food, no fluids: not even a drop of water; she would not oil or comb her hair, or use any footwear. All this was part and parcel of her strike.

The authorities could not make her eat, however hard they tried. On 21 November, the Nambol police released her, but she continued her fast in public, in Imphal.

The Porompat police arrested her the same day. They prepared to force-feed her. Sharmila's family and colleagues talked to her, in an effort to persuade her to allow force-feeding. She had been without food or fluid for several days, and was slowly fading away. They feared for her life.

Finally, they prevailed upon her. She submitted to their arguments. She accepted that losing her life without attaining her goal would not help the cause. So, she allowed herself to be nasally fed.

Slim plastic tubes have helped her survive physically, through the subsequent years. A tube was fitted internally, from nose to stomach. Another, detachable, was fitted externally from her nose, through which fluids could be poured in.

She was released from jail within a few days—on 30 December 2000. She chose to remain in the public eye rather than return home, continuing her protest in the open. She went to the Meira Paibi Shanglen, a shelter home in Kongpal Kongkham Leikai, her own neighbourhood in Imphal East. Several family members visited her, but her mother did not come; Sharmila did not want her mother to come.

She felt that meeting her mother might weaken her resolve. Shakhi Devi too felt she may grow very upset seeing her daughter's suffering, and that this in turn might greatly disturb Sharmila. Over the next years, both mother and daughter continued to feel this way. In April 2007, Shakhi Devi had not met her youngest daughter for over six years; she said, 'I think of Sharmila and feel ... sometimes I feel I will go mad.' Mother and daughter have not met for nearly fifteen years now!

T

In early January 2001, Sharmila was rearrested under a suo moto case, and kept under custody by Porompat police. The investigating officer submitted a charge sheet, and cognizance was taken under section 309, Indian Penal Code (IPC), that is 'Attempt to Suicide'. She was remanded to judicial custody, and kept behind bars for nearly a year.

She was released on 21 November 2001. Porompat police promptly arrested her again, on 24 November. The next time they released her was 2 August 2002, but again she was re-arrested almost immediately. The following day, she was produced in court and once again remanded to judicial custody. In the year 2003 Sharmila was released but again arrested and remanded to judicial custody until 6 February 2004.

All these years, she was kept in Jawaharlal Nehru (JN) Hospital, Imphal, in the Security Wing, which is administered by Sajiwa Central Jail. There was no regular time allowed for visitors. People keen to visit her, had to apply for permission from the home ministry. Often, permission was not granted. Sharmila was condemned, in effect, to a solitary existence. Home Guards and nurses were under instructions to behave strictly with her.

On 6 February 2004, the medical superintendent, JN Hospital (hospital of the Jawaharlal Nehru Institute of Medical Sciences, JNIMS), Imphal, wrote a letter to the additional superintendent, Sajiwa Central Jail requesting that Sharmila be shifted away from the hospital. The same day, the jail's additional superintendent made an application to the civil judge, Manipur, for releasing Sharmila from judicial custody. The next day the civil judge passed an order allowing her release from custody on furnishing a personal bond.

She could well have availed of this order, moved out of jail and lived as a free person. But she refused to do this, since it would imply an apology, and a giving up of her fast. The personal bond would really be a promise that she would not continue with her 'crime'. She never considered this, not for a moment. Through all the long and lonely years, her single-minded determination did not falter.

𑀝

Human Rights Law Network (HRLN), New Delhi, took the initiative to advise Sharmila to approach the Supreme Court of India for unconditional release. On 14 February 2004, Irom Sharmila approached the Supreme Court. The Supreme Court dismissed her petition on 30 April because it had bypassed the high court, but encouraged her to use her liberty to avail of legal remedies.

Her case had, by now, received attention from organizations in different parts of the world. Here is a telling excerpt from the section on 'Human Rights Defenders', in the chapter on 'Promotion and Protection of Human Rights', within UNESCO's *Commission on Human Rights, 2003*:[29]

> Report submitted by Ms Hina Jilani, Special Representative of the Secretary-General on human rights defenders, in accordance with Commission on Human Rights Resolution 2000/61

Communication received

> By letter dated 22 October 2002, the Government replied to the urgent appeal sent on 19 January 2001 regarding Irom Sharmila ... The Government informed the Special Representative that Ms. Sharmila was arrested

on 24 November 2001 'while she was trying to commit suicide by fasting to death at PDA Complex at Porompat near J.N. Hospital, Imphal under Porompat P.S. She was demanding the removal of Armed Forces Special Powers Act (Assam and Manipur, 1958) from the State of Manipur'. With clearance from the medical officer from J.N. Hospital, Ms. Sharmila was formally arrested. The same day she was produced before the Court of Chief Judicial Magistrate, Imphal. While in police custody, Ms. Sharmila was interrogated. According to the authorities she disclosed that she had been convicted earlier for the same offence by the magistrate at Imphal East. Thus it is apparent that Irom Sharmila was a habitual offender who had been frequently trying to commit suicide by fasting unto death. On 24 November 2001 the Chief Magistrate of Imphal ordered her remanded into judicial custody for 15 days. As per the instructions of the court, she was administered nasal feeding at J.N. Hospital before being taken to jail. She has since been held in custody in Manipur Central Jail, Sajiwa. On 5 March 2002 a medical officer found that her condition was stable.

Observations

The Special Representative thanks the Government for its reply. She regrets, however, that at the time of finalisation of the present report, no response had been received from the Government to her other more recent communications.

On 9 September 2004, she was released, but immediately re-arrested. On 16 September a colleague filed a petition in the High Court, Guwahati, for her unconditional release. On 21 September the High Court passed an order directing the state government to forthwith release Irom Sharmila unless her custody is required in any other case. A copy of this order (dated 21 September 2004) was furnished to the Manipur government by her counsel on 27 September. Two days later, that is, on 29 September 2004, Sharmila was released in compliance with the court order. However, the very next day she was re-arrested by Porompat police in another case, with the same charge of attempt to suicide, and produced in court. The court again remanded her to judicial custody!

Well into the fifth year of her protest, Irom Sharmila was released on 1 October 2005, only to be re-arrested the same day, from the open ground where she continued her fast. She was produced before the magistrate the next day and was remanded to judicial custody.

By now the pattern was clear. The government would treat her as a habitual criminal, arrest and keep her in judicial custody for several months or up to a year, release, and then re-arrest her. She would be tried, and subjected to the same rigmarole. This became a regular routine.

REDEFINING DEVELOPMENT

Irom Sharmila has always maintained she will give up her fast as soon as AFSPA is withdrawn. Her immediate cause is clear: she has reiterated it often. But her deeper motivations go beyond any simplistic one-point programme. From the central point of repealing AFSPA in Manipur, her goals spread in concentric circles. She demands political accountability, economic welfare and educational opportunities for all. She upholds plural cultural identities and ecological lifestyles, and an end to violence of all types, at every level. She redefines development, well beyond the dominant paradigm which focuses on quantitative economic growth. Her definition, in line with many alternative thinkers and activists, is of development as oriented towards basic human needs, sustainable and empowering *for all*. Such development is essential to realize peace and justice in the world.

Implicitly, Irom Sharmila poses a civilizational challenge. She is critiquing dominant paradigms of modernity and development, and suggesting that we must fashion other, very different, modes of human life and livelihood. Her vision includes preservation of traditional indigenous wisdom, adapted creatively to diverse cultural and technological changes flowing in from the rest of the world.

Her campaign is not limited to one state, or one country.

Its intent is universal. It is a reassertion of human dignity and inner strength, in the face of militarism and brute power.

Her one demand is symbolic: it signifies a turning of the current. Withdrawal of AFSPA would mean that politicians are willing to begin responding to the real issues faced by the common person. There are links between rampant violence and lack of people-oriented development. Sharmila is questioning the model of profit-led development, with its overexploitation of nature, breeding of consumerism, and neglect of marginalized regions. Her stand makes clear that the violence her state is experiencing is not isolated, rather it is part of a pattern: of neglect, exploitation and underdevelopment.

She traces historical continuities with the transparent imperialism of the past, noting, 'In Manipur there is no development. There is no industry. Everything is being imported. Even the rice is imported. We do not have enough agriculture to feed rice to people round the year. Earlier we had rice in plenty, but now we do not grow enough for our needs. There are no jobs, for any job a huge bribe has to be paid. My campaign is for the right kind of development. The politicians are not thinking of development. They are very selfish and corrupt. When I thought of taking this step, it was to change the trend in politics. I took this step, because I cannot accept the politics in our state, it is so dirty. Politicians should work for the people, but they are not doing so.'[30]

She seeks to influence contemporary policy, draw attention to gross travesties of justice, and bring forward an alternative path. This alternative would ensure that everybody's basic needs are met, and human rights respected. It would attend to a revival of agriculture, appropriate industrialization, relevant education and dignified livelihoods. Local planning and wisdom would guide development, and common people would be encouraged to come together to work for change. She is concerned about preserving nature, and maintaining cultural integrity.

She is well aware that Manipur has inherited a troubled legacy. The ghost of colonialism has not been laid to rest; the forcible merger with India has not been forgotten. Memories of ancient glory lurk just beneath the surface, adding fuel to popular dissatisfaction.

During British rule, a self-sufficient, proud and independent kingdom was reduced to a condition of dependence. It lost self-sufficiency in food, and people's livelihoods could no longer meet their basic needs. This trend has intensified with time. Rather than development, Manipur is experiencing the 'development of underdevelopment'. Globalization is fostering this process, by creating conditions for attracting capital to regions where there is cheap labour and land, minerals and oil. Manipur possesses rich resources, as do many other 'backward' regions of the country. The trend today, led by hard-nosed profit-oriented capitalist corporations and national governments, is to extract and exploit the resources, without paying adequate recompense. The 'backward' regions are thus rendered more, rather than less, 'backward'.

During colonial rule, wealth and resources were drained away from the colonies, to the colonizer nations. The Indian economy was manipulated, leading to decline in agriculture, traditional industries and crafts, and other indigenous systems. Raw materials were whisked away and people de-skilled, resulting in impoverishment. Similar policies continue under Indian rule. The subsistence economy continues to crumble. No significant employment opportunities have been created. Barely any infrastructure has developed for the welfare of the local populace.

While the colonial regime manipulated paddy sales, today the state and corporate sector are eyeing natural gas, oil and uranium. Manipuris allege that New Delhi divides and rules in Manipur to empty entire areas of the state. Manipur conceals a real treasury: 'Imphal is sitting on natural gas and uranium,' explains Ajita, an ordinary citizen. She adds that under Manipuri soil there is 'black gold'—oil.[31]

Marginalized regions like Manipur are victims of internal colonization, a veritable 'Fourth World' whose resources are exploited without providing due returns. As Seram Rojesh, ex-president of the Manipuri Students' Union, Delhi, puts it, 'There has been no development in Manipur since independence. Even under the British there was not so much exploitation.'[32]

Manipur, and other north-eastern states, have abundant timber and other forest resources. The Centre looks upon this region as a source of revenue, and as a conduit for trade between mainland India and South-East Asia. The Look East Policy (LEP), in place since 1992, is meant to promote better land route connections with South-East Asia, facilitating access to various commodities, for instance, Myanmar's extensive energy reserves.

Mr Nobo Kishore, well-known social worker and director of Centre for Social Development (CSD), an Imphal-based NGO, explains, 'It is in order to intensify exploitation that the Indian state physically dominates in Manipur. This is the real reason that the army and paramilitary forces are sent in here. It is to maintain "law and order" if people question the exploitation of their land and resources. It is to keep the people quiet.'

༒

Irom Sharmila's stand is in consonance with a worldwide search for alternative modes of development. Instead of denouncing and rejecting indigenous ways of life and thought, people seeking 'alternatives' are looking to assimilate the best from tradition and from modernity, even as society moves forward. Her position gently reminds us that the future is not to be devoid of ethical and political commitments.

In Manipur's traditional subsistence economy, people's labour in fields, forests, handlooms and local markets was generally sufficient to provide for a good life. The state was self-sufficient in essentials such as paddy, cotton, vegetables, fish, bamboo and other forest products. People cultivated and processed their own cotton. Weaving continues to be an important occupation today, but only a paltry income accrues to the weavers.[33] Cotton cultivation died out in Manipur under colonial policy, and the Indian government has not seen it fit to rejuvenate cotton farms. Manipuri weavers now buy imported yarn. They have no option, although prices have skyrocketed in recent years. Women producers dye the yarn, weave beautiful patterns, and sell small quantities of fabric in the local market. Tragically, their income today is insufficient for family survival.

Trade and commerce are largely in the hands of settlers, brought in under deliberate colonial policy. These 'outsider' businessmen control transport, storage and communication, and dominate the economy. Economic power in the hands of local women and men has declined.

The number of people below the poverty line in Manipur has risen. Today, in this erstwhile self-sufficient society, 140,500 people are estimated to live below the poverty line.[34] Unemployment is severe in rural and urban areas, for the educated as well as the illiterate. Substantial numbers of educated youth are jobless. In 2002, as many as 414,800 people were registered in the employment exchange.[35] Rampant unemployment has led to widespread frustration and alienation amongst the youth. In the capital city, hundreds of 'educated' rickshaw drivers move about with their faces wrapped in cloth, eyes peering out through slits.

There is a widespread feeling of insecurity and a scramble for scarce opportunities, resources and jobs. At stake is the basic well-being of families, clans and communities. As groups confront threats to survival, self-esteem and identity, they become defensive, and often misdirect their anger against one another. A blame game begins, and takes on its own momentum. Rigid identity politics is a result of this crisis. Ethnic rivalries have sharpened in Manipur, during the past decades, to the point of violent conflagrations.

Thus despite becoming a full-fledged state, life has not improved for the common people of Manipur. Misguided priorities occupy centre stage. Reduced to a puppet in the hands of the Central government, its agriculture continues to languish, industry is virtually non-existent, education and health systems limp along.

Parties in power in Delhi have flooded Manipur with funds, but in so doing deliberately created a coterie of contractors, who take 95 per cent of the funds back to Delhi. Even government sources acknowledge that useful developmental projects have not come to fruition, while the black market has prospered.[36] Daily life has grown increasingly hard, with scarcity of essential commodities and widespread discontent.

People are resisting projects slated to destroy vast tracts of forest, villages and agricultural land, which result in displacement and ecological destruction. Agriculture and allied activities like animal husbandry, horticulture, pisciculture and forestry still engage 80 per cent of the workforce, but are threatened by myopic state policies. Thus, for instance, the Loktak Multipurpose Hydroelectric Power Project in 1984 led to inundation of nearly 50,000 hectares of arable land along the Loktak wetlands. Presently, 207 hectares of fertile land is being acquired for modernization of Imphal's Tulihal airport, displacing some 250 families from Malom, Ningombam, Meitram, Kodompokpi, Mongsangei and Konjeng Leikai villages. As Deejen Khoisnam, joint secretary of the Joint Action Committee (JAC) against Acquisition of Land for Airport Expansion, points out: 'Any further alienation of land is likely to swell the ranks of the poor, and give a fillip to insurgency.' On 2 April 2008, there was a confrontation between protesters and the police.[37]

The controversial Mapithel Dam project lacks any environmental assessment or rehabilitation plans, and is riddled with corruption. The Irrigation and Flood Control Department, Government of Manipur, has speeded up construction of this dam, despite consistent opposition by people. By insisting on the dam, 'IFCD continues to defy people's repeated call for sustainable development ...' A civil society organization,

Citizens' Concern for Dams and Development (CCDD), asserts: 'Gaining public acceptance is essential for decisions on equitable and sustainable water and energy resources development.' Acceptance will emerge if projects are designed with due recognition to survival issues, habitat protection and human rights.[38]

Like CCDD, Irom Sharmila represents a viewpoint that is totally opposed to environmental destruction, corporate greed and unbridled consumerism. In her perspective, development ought to be attuned to nature, ecological and sustainable. She advocates development that respects health and welfare, unlike the dominant developmental mode. In 'developed' areas, in the name of food people now consume toxic chemicals, which have leeched into soil, water and air—by-products of a system obsessed with private profiteering.

Thus she takes a clear and unequivocal stand against the unilinear developmental model propagated by a globalized economy, which is really a form of continuing imperialism. She underlines the importance of diversity and plurality. Distinct cultural identities are important. They should not be divisive, but at the same time they should not be ignored or flattened out. A homogenized world is anathema to millions of people who exhibit an immense variety of beliefs, customs and lifestyles. Many indigenous cultures have elements that ought to be preserved, being strongly imbued with ecological, aesthetic, ethical and social values.

Her anti-AFSPA stand draws critical attention to the need to protect our democratic rights and civil liberties. Democracy is yet to become true democracy, faithful to its own Constitution. People's participation, an empty rhetoric as of now, will be achieved only when people struggle for it.

Intrinsic to her world view is the notion of cosmic balance, and the awareness that human beings are not masters of nature. 'We learn everything from nature,' she reminds us, in her firm, soft tones. Human culture and economy must be redesigned, to harmonize with the natural world. We are passing residents in this world, not its owners. Her thinking is in consonance with traditional wisdom as well as postmodern ethics—and opposed to the arrogant modernist belief that human beings are masters of nature, which they can alter, destroy, use and abuse.

Irom Sharmila does not argue that everything in indigenous culture is worthy of protection. Wherever there are inequalities, ugliness, sectarianism or elitism, these should be shed. Cooperation, simple living and hard work, with due recompense for all kinds of labour, should be basic to the new social and economic order. If she were to have her way, a basic commitment to mutuality, sustainability and non-violence would form the backbone of culture, society and politics—across the world.

As she continues her fast, Sharmila has herself become a touchstone, an anchor, a reminder that a better world is possible. Her continuing struggle encourages others to speak up on multiple issues, work for an end to violence, and imagine alternative futures.

WOMEN'S SOLIDARITY: MOVEMENT AGAINST RAPE

Women continue to be a strong force against violence. With a long tradition of women's solidarity and powerful movements against colonialism and state violence, Manipuri women are living up to their rich heritage. They are at the forefront of struggles against atrocities committed upon ordinary people. As part of this commitment, they have taken up cudgels against state violence on women. Sharmila's determined protest against AFSPA, and state violence blessed by AFSPA, draws incalculable support from the widespread community of women activists. In fact, millions of ordinary women in Manipur are activists, in one way or another.

When Irom Sharmila sat on fast against the Malom killings, on 5 November 2000, senior Meira Paibi women were the first to embrace her struggle as their own. They sat with her in solidarity—providing a passionate, empathetic understanding. Seasoned activists like Ima Mangol, Ima Taruni and Ima Ramani as well as many others have throughout extended wholehearted support to the younger woman—'our daughter', as they frequently refer to her.

'Today Manipur is surviving only because of its Imas,' says Rojesh, while accompanying me to meet senior Meira Paibi activists in Imphal, in 2006. Such a frankly respectful estimation of the political worth of elderly women is a refreshing change from the cynical misogyny typical of north India. Here in the North-East I come across young male activists, neither macho nor self-aggrandizing, actually assessing and honouring the overwhelming role played by women in the survival of their society.

Irom Sharmila, as crusader for justice and peace, is associated with this heritage. Women activists in Manipur are usually projected as 'Imas'—quintessentially elderly mother figures: Sharmila is an honourable exception.

Elderly working-class women—peasants, traders and vendors—have formed the substratum for collective resistance over the centuries. This historical fact is critical to Sharmila's trajectory as an activist. In adopting a non-violent mode of struggle, Nisha Bandhis and Meira Paibis have been her leaders, and sisters, in struggle. Like Meira Paibis, she clearly rejects the violent modes of protest represented by many insurgent groups.

She takes an uncompromising stand against violence, whether by insurgents or by the state. Insurgency distorts civilian life, which is further threatened by widespread militarization. As violence percolates deeper into the social structure, most women suffer increased vulnerability, deprivation and physical assault.

☡

Armed forces deployed in the North-East have used violence and abuse as weapons of control, symbols of humiliation and threat to local communities. Rehabilitation and compensation have been absent or negligible.[39] Patriarchal ideology insists that extremely high levels of violence are 'normal'. This ideology flows into militaristic mentality, which glorifies practices associated with war and the military, including the celebration of routine violence. Destructive weapons are construed as legitimate, and murder, even genocide, justified. When soldiers rape 'the enemy's women', it is valorized as the ultimate victory, signifying an extreme of humiliation.

In Manipur, militaristic mentality has taken charge. The use of violence is justified and glorified, by both insurgents and state representatives. Both sides use violence indiscriminately, leading to an endless spiral. The armed forces are increasingly unleashing violence upon the populace, including sexual violence upon women.

Crimes committed by security forces in recent years, in Manipur, include rapes, such as of Ms Nandeibam Sanjita of Uchathol Jiribam, by 12th Grenadier Rifles, on 4 October 2003.[40] By the turn of the century, murder, torture, arrests and rape had become the order of the day. People had grown familiar with the taste of fear. But they were not resigned to it: they refused to accept the situation.

Popular resentment burst into flame when people heard of a new atrocity: the rape and murder of Ms Thangjam Manorama of Bamon Kampu, by 17th Assam Rifles personnel, during 11 and 12 July 2004.

On 15 July 2004, Meira Paibi activists staged a dramatic protest against this rape. Their radical action exposed state protection of the criminals. The protest refused to accept a militarized, violent order that converts any and all women into victims. The protesters articulated the anger and pain of millions of ordinary women. What happened to Thangjam

Manorama Devi of Bamon Kampu, Imphal, could happen to any woman, in a militarized world.

On 11 July 2004, 17th Assam Rifles personnel broke down the door of Thangjam Manorama's house, dragged her out of bed and assaulted her elderly mother and two younger brothers who tried to intervene. They dragged her to a veranda, blindfolded, tied and brutally assaulted her. They threw water on her face while assaulting her for hours. Then they came in, took a kitchen knife, and looted Rs 5,000 and jewellery from the house. They forced the traumatized family to sign a 'No Claims Certificate', which stated that security men had not damaged any property or misbehaved with women folk. They gave the family an arrest memo stating Manorama was arrested on suspicion of having links with PLA. They took her away. Later that day, her partly clothed, mutilated corpse was found dumped by the side of a road. Villagers who found her said there were scratch marks all over the body, a gashing knife wound on her right thigh, deep cuts on thighs and genitals, bruises on breasts, and several bullet wounds. The Irilbung police picked up her body, and the Regional Institute of Medical Sciences conducted an autopsy. The autopsy report was not released to the family or public.

People's anger erupted, in a protest of unprecedented intensity. The bereaved family demanded an official inquiry into the murder. Twelve Meira Paibi women protested in the nude, outside the massive wrought-iron gates of Kangla Fort, where several regiments of Assam Rifles were stationed. The women took off their phaneks and blouses in public, carrying a long white banner with the blood-smeared slogan emblazoned on it—*INDIAN ARMY, RAPE US*. Shouting,

'Rape Us, Kill Us, Take Our Flesh', these protesters tried to break into the Assam Rifles headquarters, Kangla.

The women's nude protest captured the headlines in various newspapers. It drew public attention, in and outside Manipur. Due to this courageous act by a group of women, people in different parts of the world heard of the sufferings caused by militarization and state violence in Manipur. The nude protest was a bold act, a sacrifice requiring enormous courage.

The government imposed curfew, but civil society organizations demanded that the autopsy report be made public, and questioned why no women personnel were present when Assam Rifles 'arrested' Manorama. Citizens, activists and intellectuals formed a 'Committee against the Brutal Killing of Th Manorama Devi by 17 AR'. The Committee carried out a thorough investigation, after which it clarified to the public that Manorama was an innocent civilian who had no connection with any insurgents or underground organizations operating in the state.

Manipur's chief minister, O. Ibobi Singh, had to face public ire, and respond to their challenges. He admitted there was no improvement in law and order since AFSPA was imposed in 1980, and agreed to a judicial inquiry into the Manorama case. The inquiry was subsequently conducted, but its report never made public.[41]

Due to the women's protest, Sriprakash Jaiswal, Union minister of state for home, promised to vacate the historic Kangla Fort. He also promised to set afoot a review of AFSPA. He stated that in future the army would use women personnel whenever action is initiated against a female suspect. Most people felt that he made the promises only in order to quell the ongoing public protest. All the same, these were important steps in the long march towards justice in Manipur.

ॐ

Loitam Ibetombi Devi, one of the brave protesters, explains what pushed the elderly women to imagine and undertake such a difficult action: 'Our humiliation was beyond endurance,' she notes, recounting several instances of excesses by security forces. Women were not willing to take it any more. They wanted to express this in unequivocal terms. They could not condone or ignore what had happened, so they took action. They took to the streets, in order to expose and humiliate the rapists. Yet, though their intention was crystal clear, they risked social stigma and criticism from self-appointed guardians of patriarchal ethical codes. For instance, a litterateur later commented that he is 'sceptical about the moral justifiability of the act'.[42] Most sections of people in Manipur, however, strongly supported the women's action.

Ima Gyaneswari, another of the twelve leading protesters, explains that despite being extremely traditional, she joined the protest because it was a do-or-die situation for the women of Manipur. Her husband and sons later reconciled to the fact that what she did was indeed courageous.[43] Meira Paibis explain that often in the past, women have been raped by armed forces in front of their children, parents and other family members. This time they decided to stand up against the atrocity.[44]

As soon as they heard of the rape-cum-murder of Thangjam Manorama, about fifty senior women activists held a meeting, on the night of 14 July 2004. They sent out a call for a sit-in protest, to all Meira Paibis and the public at large. Alongside, they planned the nude protest. Next morning, hundreds of people arrived to participate in the sit-in at Mapal Kangjeibung, the enormous polo ground which has since long been the major venue for people's protests in Imphal. The army, however, dispersed the protesters. A bunch of women then set off for Kangla Gate, which is very close by. They were following the course of action they had planned the previous night.

One of the twelve nude protesters notes, 'Our anger made us shed our inhibitions that day. If necessary we will die—commit self-immolation to save our innocent sons and daughters ... We have nothing to do with the underground organizations. Our struggle is to protect the people caught in the crossfire between militants and security forces. We are neither protecting militants nor fighting security forces. Our only concern is the safety of our children. Our fight is to protect human rights which are being misused under AFSPA.'[45]

Through their spirited protest, the women exposed the dirty underbelly of militarism, in democratic India. When law turns a blind eye to rape and murder, it reveals itself as 'unlawful' law. It is untenable, and must change. If the intention behind posting security forces is to protect people against violence, this purpose is definitely not being fulfilled.

Strong resistance indicates people's refusal to accept a regime that victimizes them. By their extraordinarily courageous action, women have brought one rape, and the context in which it could take place with impunity, to world attention. They initiated dialogue with all concerned, on the major issues involved. Their action created a liminal space through which the issues at stake could be reformulated. They pushed the state onto the defensive. By creating new symbolic frames for complex realities, the nude protest urged flexibility in addressing problems and seeking resolutions. The protest could not by itself negotiate a solution, but it certainly did create a new way forward.

Women wrested a position of strength, transforming themselves in one quicksilver moment, from total victims to determined survivors. They helped people reconnect with subjugated identities—as women, and as Manipuris—from the new position of strength. Their 'ritual of inversion' enabled those at the margins of power to dilute the impact of power and even, momentarily, turn power relations upside down. By this temporary inversion, people gained new perspectives. Through symbolically enacting collective power, it became possible to imagine an enduring struggle that would confront and transform abuse. Such a perspective has the ability to last, tenacious beyond the momentary public protest.[46]

Coupled with Irom Sharmila's continuing fast, the nude protest against state rape has formed the bulwark for protests against AFSPA. Between them they have woven a strong fabric, with patterns that reflect human imagination, and indicate that there might indeed be space to recreate society and state anew.

BODY POLITICS:
TWO UNIQUE PROTESTS

Sharmila's protest is an integral part of the tapestry of struggle being woven by countless Manipuri women and men. One voice of dissent among other voices, she has place of honour in a long line of fierce resistors. As crime piles upon crime in her blood-struck land, her resolve is unflagging. Her determination grows only stronger.

Both the anti-rape action and Sharmila's fast come across as unique, non-violent and powerful forms of protest. Their ends are the same—to stop violence under AFSPA or any other brutal law. Both forms of protest have used the power of the human body to mould, formulate and transmit messages, communicating important truths.

In their anger and the skill evolved as seasoned activists, the Meira Paibis forged a creative way of struggle. By disrobing in public, they challenged the division of private and public spheres, and the secrecy with which 'private' matters are supposed to be treated. Perceiving rape to be intrinsically political—a crime asserting power—they publicly identified state security forces as the perpetrators, and challenged the state to own up to its crime. They demanded transparency and accountability. The state claims to protect people from crime:

it must launch an investigation and punish the perpetrators, *especially* if the perpetrators are state employees.

The protesters assigned dishonour to those males who violate, who commit heinous crimes, and the state that protects them—skilfully inverting the usual association of dishonour with women's violated bodies.

They asserted their interpretation of rape, an interpretation respectful of women's integrity and rights. They clearly distanced themselves from the usual patriarchal definition of rape, as dishonour to family and community. Rather than speak of dishonour to community or family, their discourse focussed on the violation of one woman as symbolic of, or even tantamount to, the violation of all women. They emphasized solidarity and commonalities between different women. Graphically, they conveyed vulnerability as well as strength through the force of their nudity. Their public disrobing indicated that in the contemporary ethos, all women are treated like lambs for slaughter: any woman can be picked up, tortured, raped and killed. And yet, women do not accept this treatment, will not submit to such violation.

The sheer genius of the Meira Paibis lay in evolving, and actually practising, this difficult mode of struggle. By deliberately exposing their bodies, the women asserted their right to their own bodies. Rejecting the masculinist definition of women's bodies as attractive or unattractive, available or unavailable, they moved into an entirely different paradigm. Women's bodies, in this radical paradigm, are not others' to possess. They are not objects of male gaze, or what is more extreme, male violation. Rather, the body is a woman's means of expression—of intelligence, anger, dissent, resistance, fearlessness. The women consciously created a collective expression of rage, challenging concentrated, brutal patriarchal power. It was the first time in recorded history that women collectively used their bodies in this manner.

Shouting 'Indian Army, Rape Us, Take Our Flesh' was a spirited challenge to the security forces, an exposé of crimes committed in secrecy. Everybody 'knew' security personnel had committed the crime, yet the state refused to acknowledge culpability. Law-abiding citizens were furious with the lawlessness and hypocrisy of the state. The nude protesters inverted male logic, used irony and black humour, to bring out the truth everybody already knew: the 'naked truth'. In their rage vis-à-vis the crime, they mocked the criminals, challenging them to commit the crime again, as it were, in full public glare.

In patriarchal society, women's bodies are controlled by male-defined structures. Men 'own' women's bodies, stamp these with their own names and lineages, desires and demands. The nude protest challenged all of this. Women's bodies are *not* objects of male desire, control or manipulation. The protesters insisted that women were the true owners of their own bodies: the arbiters of the body's destiny. When this principle is violated by force, by a man or by a state, women do not submit, do not accept. They object, raise their voices, protest in the most flagrant manner possible.

The nude protesters were ordinary women: Imas, housewives, traders, professionals. Other women easily related to them. Their bodies were not the caricatures of ideal feminine beauty sold by commercial dream factories, cosmetic and media industries. They were not figures sculpted to feed predatory fantasy. Strong women, flesh surging in anger, they were expressing themselves, rather than feeding patriarchy. They reclaimed their agency: the right to be respected as thinking, articulate, autonomous subjects.

Patriarchy condemns raped women to social ostracism. Rape becomes her badge of shame, a marker for life. The Imas publicly refused to accept this. They protested on behalf of all women, all human beings, and particularly for the younger generation of women. They spoke in defence of their daughters, the younger women like Manorama, who are central to globalized patriarchal fantasies. They spoke deliberately, controlling and orchestrating their rage, which was a reaction to violence suffered over the generations. The public protest was their reply, their challenge. It was a message of enduring, endless resistance.

༦

Like the twelve Imas, Irom Sharmila has fielded her body as a weapon. It is a deliberate, well-thought-out move. By fasting without end, she is asserting her right to deploy her body as she sees fit. She is expressing her resistance to injustice and the 'lawless law' through defiant inversion of the norm—of eating food. Eating daily meals is so basic to human beings, and a central ritual of human society, that refusing to do so strikes a blow to the whole system.

She says, 'I am not a spirit. I have a body. It has a metabolism.' Like any of us, she is a person with a body, mind and heart. As a composite entity, she takes decisions regarding her self. She can protest through her body—making, if she so chooses, a sacrifice. If she does not eat, it is not so as to die. True, the body must be fed in order to survive. She allows artificial feeding methods, though not fully reconciled to doing so.

Her main strategy remains untouched: refusal to eat in the natural, normal way.

Not a drop of water has passed her lips these fourteen years since November 2000. She has not combed her hair, worn footwear, or looked into a mirror. All these, she denies herself.

Force-feeding is a practical and tactical compromise, and as such, it troubles her. She enquires, in anguish and confusion, 'Why do they feed me? They are not my mother and father.' The paradox is literally unsolvable. She wants the state to engage in dialogue with her, but it refuses. Instead, it arrests and imprisons her on spurious grounds. And yet, it keeps her alive. She could not otherwise have survived the rigours of a continuous fast, and would have starved to death years ago. She submits to force-feeding because she is *not* in fact seeking martyrdom. As she puts it, she is 'in no mood for suicide'. She is seeking only to further the people's cause, push ahead the campaign against AFSPA.

In campaigning endlessly, indefinitely, she has become a constant thorn in the flesh of her opponents. In undertaking voluntary suffering in her flesh, she is creating psychological discomfort in her opponents. Symbolically, she is saying, 'See, an ordinary person has nothing in today's social system. I have only my body. But at least this, which is mine, I will use fully.'

She perceives the protest fast as her duty, a commitment. Any harm her body may incur is, in her view, inconsequential. Rather than submit to weakness or disease, Irom Sharmila chooses to be a fighter, a survivor in her own unique way. As she puts it, speaking to me in November 2006, 'I have no other power. I do not have economic power, or political power. I have only my self. This is the only way I have to get my voice heard.'

Here is a person exercising her right over her body, and over the way she chooses to live. She communicates her message in no uncertain terms. We understand that this person refuses to be quiescent while injustice and violence rage all around. She speaks out resistance, through every pore of her being.

In judicial custody year after year, she has not allowed anybody to make her taste a morsel of food, or indeed a drop of water. She submits to the tough and uncomfortable regime of the plastic tube.

She remains steadfast, gentle and attentive; listening or reading, her mind active. She speaks selectively in intense, measured prose. Her emotions and ideas overflow into lines of rhythmic verse. Although she greatly enjoys the company of friends, solitary detention has been her lot for many years now. She accepts her suffering with stoic calm, realizing that it is unavoidable.

When others express concern about the effect on her physical health, she says, 'That doesn't matter. We are all mortal.' To her mind, this is not an infliction. It is not a punishment. It is simply her bounden duty.

She experiments continually with her body—through yoga and walking. She is exceptionally close to nature, and the work with her body is in harmony with the rhythms of nature. Although she is fasting indefinitely, her daily practice of yoga has kept her in fairly good health. She feels that, with regular yoga, she might live thus for even a hundred years. She says, 'Yoga is not like football. It is different. If a person does yoga, it can help one to live longer. By doing yoga, one can live up to one hundred years! It is not so with other sports, like football.'

She sees the body and human beings per se, as part of nature, subject to natural laws. She upholds exercises which nurture the body's inner wisdom, providing good health and longevity. This is in consonance with ecologically sound development, respecting the earth and nature's rhythms.

There is a sense of urgency about her struggle. The world is hurtling towards self-destruction, and the only way to save it is to pause, step back, and refuse to cooperate with the madness: listening instead to the small voice within each of us, which points towards better directions. Listening to the voice of sanity alerts us to the pressing need to take a stand, clarify and articulate our position, and to do so now. It is time to press 'Stop': stop militarism now. Stop state violence now. Stop the crazy arms race now. Stop polluting the earth, producing junk for profit, and unrestrained consumerism. Put people first: now!

The struggle can neither be abandoned, nor postponed. It demands as much as we can give it: flesh and blood, body and soul, a minute, a day, or a lifetime.

SOUL-FORCE AND
NON-VIOLENCE

Out of nearly 200 forms of non-violent resistance,[47] contemporary peace scholars characterize fasting as among the most important. Most protesters fast only for strategic ends, using this method as a tactical tool. Their aim is direct and unambiguous: the fast is meant to obtain a particular goal by exposing and shaming perpetrators of injustice, and pressurizing them to end their unjust ways. The oppressors may remain ethically unconvinced, yet under duress act in a manner desired by the protester. This method is commonly used by people to achieve immediate ends.

Others—like Irom Sharmila—express a deeper world view through this method. Fasting, for such protesters, is an act of 'philosophical non-violence'. Sharmila's goals are multilayered. Though her fast is political, tactical and strategic, it is at the same time an integral part of a deeper process of ethical discipline. It is a means of non-violent expression, which not only trains one's own self but is also designed to teach the 'opponent', bringing about a change of heart, a conversion in terms of ethical beliefs and convictions.

Irom Sharmila's immediate strategic goal is visible, the withdrawal of AFSPA, but underlying it is an effort to sensitize people, including government and policy makers, in a deeper way. It aims to bring about a radical change in political ethos and thinking, towards respect for human rights, appropriate development, fulfilment of basic needs and cultural integrity. Through this transformation, she seeks to restore order in the state of Manipur.

Sharmila often refers to her fast as a 'spiritual' act. It bears a kinship to the numerous fasts kept by Mahatma Gandhi. The method is not easy, as it demands total dedication, at the cost of one's own health and, indeed, freedom.

She explains that her fast is, 'For the sake of my motherland. Unless and until they remove the Armed Forces (Special Powers) Act 1958, I shall never stop fasting.'

She adds, about the future: 'I do have hope. My stand is for the sake of truth, and I believe truth succeeds eventually. God gives me courage. That is why I am still alive through these artificial means ...'[48]

Speaking for truth by using her body as her weapon, she accepts and adapts to deprivation and pain. Suffering is part of the deal, and in order to bear it, she has to develop willpower and endurance. She claims, however, that it is not very hard, since she is doing exactly what she has chosen to do—her unique task in the world. As she puts it, 'How shall I explain it, we all come here with a task to do. And we come here alone.'

So this is not just a political task, it is a vocation, a fulfilment of her destiny. She is immersed in the larger picture, within which her fast is inevitable, if she chooses to remain true to her highest aims. It is from this awareness that she draws solace and immense confidence. At the same time, she is sensitive and humane, vulnerable to emotion.

Acknowledging that emotions have the power to sway her, she has decided not to meet her mother during her fast. She knows that her mother may be unable to see her suffering, although in principle she is supportive. Sharmila explains, 'My mother knows everything about my decision. Although she is illiterate, and very simple, she has the courage to let me do my bounden duty ... There is an understanding between us: that she will meet me only after I have fulfilled my mission.'

Irom Sharmila did not choose this method as a member of any group. She belongs to no particular organization, has no exclusive affiliations. She represents no 'line'; she represents only her own conscience. Yet, her individual decision has placed her in harmony with the collective will. She has chosen to position herself entirely in the public realm, as an activist committed to achieving the common good. She is a free radical, open to the world, invested in no separate personal life of a kind that might dilute her commitments. Her family in fact helped build the vital ethical core within her, which makes her such a committed public protester for the cause of justice.

She sees herself as a symbol of justice, a rational being who represents universal truth. Her conception of universal truth is close to the Gandhian notion of truth. Gandhi's struggle for swaraj, while aiming to establish self-rule, was also a quest for the universal truth—a search for the underlying commonality that unites human beings.[49]

Gandhi went on public fast several times. The method involved self-discipline and sacrifice, which he thought would touch the hearts of his co-protesters. He undertook his first public fast during the Ahmedabad millworkers' strike, upon observing the confusion and despair of several workers. He fasted not to coerce the mill owners, rather to help build the strength and moral fibre of the workers, and consolidate their struggle. The decision to fast came to him in a flash, as he mulled over the impasse. His act of self-denial moved the workers, and strengthened their resolve to continue. Their united stand finally won the day: the mill-owners lent an ear to the workers' grievances, and agreed to a substantial wage hike.

The underlying rationale behind Gandhi's frequent fasts, which were part of his lifelong 'experiments with truth', was an aspiration to control the senses and emotions, rather than be controlled by them, as is ordinarily the case. Both fasting and 'maun vratas'—days of silence—were conducive to introspection, and an essential part of his efforts to rein in greed, anger, impatience, fear and related emotions.

The Buddha frequently kept long fasts, as part of the process of self-discovery. As he meditated on the long path to self-realization, absorbed in the inner journey, eating became relatively unimportant, even (temporarily) unnecessary. Indulgence in food became a sign of continuing entrapment in the world of desires, of grasping at transient pleasures. His Middle Way did not enjoin harsh self-denial: rather food fell into its rightful place in human life: a means of sustenance to keep the body functioning, not a source of endless enjoyment. Happiness comes not from endless fulfilment of cravings, but from developing the mind, carefully selecting one's actions, and living in harmony with nature.

Most religions enjoin fasting, be it the Muslim 'roza' during which for a month the devout are to eat nothing between daybreak and dusk, not even swallow their own spit, or the

Christian Lent. In Jain, Vaishnavite and various other traditions, women keep regular fasts in the sanctity of their homes, a self-cleansing discipline, with physical and spiritual connotations. It has also been a means for voicing resistance, at different occasions and for varied purposes. A younger woman from a Jain household in central India recalls, 'My grandmother kept a weekly fast, and also fasted whenever she could not persuade the men in the family about something important. By fasting, she exerted a special moral pressure, and frequently was able to extend the argument and win the day.' Ordinary women have thus practised satyagraha, fashioning habitual fasts into tools of resistance.

Irom Sharmila regularly observed a weekly fast, as part of her personal discipline, for years. Thus fasting was by no means foreign, or new, to her. Her public fast is of course political, but at the same time it is rooted in her spiritual quest, part of her God-assigned duties, which entail endurance and self-refinement. As she says, trying to translate into mundane language the deeper mainsprings of her actions, 'I have not succeeded so far in my aim. It means that I have to purify myself. God is experimenting with me. There is so much dirt inside us! I have to cleanse myself first.'

Her fast has this special inner dimension. But it is no selfish venture, designed to win personal salvation while the rest of humanity carries on unredeemed. Her task in the world involves influencing and changing people, society and politics. Like Gandhi, an involved political actor, Sharmila's spirituality does not isolate or separate her from the common run of humanity. Rather it is a force that connects her with wider humanity, and with the cosmos.

Gandhi appealed to the humane qualities of his opponents,

to bring about a change of heart and transform them into allies. The spiritual dimension flowed into the political. Sharmila, similarly, is 'not satisfied' with superficial statements and cosmetic changes. Keen for deeper transformation, her protest is not merely for withdrawal of one law, although that is the immediate focus. Her fast aims to change the hearts and minds of people—including those who run the state and the country—radically altering their thinking and consciousness, which in turn would significantly transform their policies and behaviour.

Because of the complicated nature of her demand, and the refusal, so far, of authorities to bend or change, her fast is indefinite. She is clear that her intention is not to commit suicide, and so submits to nasal feeding as a pragmatic measure, even though it is a painful process. The tube that is thrust into her nose gives a great deal of discomfort. Fluid accumulates in her chin area as a result of nasal feeding and she has had to have surgeries to deal with the problem.

She wears her self-sacrifice lightly. Gandhi identified certain 'vratas' or vows, as integral to a non-violent social order. The most important among these are *ahimsa* (non-violence), *satya* (truth), *asteya* (refrain from stealing), *brahmacharya* (celibacy or restraint), *asangraha* (non-accumulation), *sharirashrama* (physical work), *aswad* (control of the palate), *abhaya* (fearlessness), *sarvadharma samabhava* (equal treatment for all religions), *swadeshi* (self-rule) and *sparshabhavana* (abjuring untouchability).[50] Irom Sharmila is living most of these precepts. It would be difficult to find a more sincere practitioner.

She is an intense, deeply emotional person, open to love, frank about desires, yet at the same time, convinced about the need for inner discipline. She believes that if each person controls cravings for unlimited wealth, power, fame and so on, inner peace would be enhanced, leading in turn to a more peaceful society. By curbing the free play of greed, human beings can check unbridled consumerism and misappropriation of the earth's resources.

She demonstrates a sharp contrast to the common dedication to pursue and accumulate *things*. The only things Sharmila has, apart from essential clothing, are books. This voluntary minimization of possessions is a radical departure from the acquisitive tendencies that are dominant today. Even with books, she prefers to borrow rather than buy. She practises aswad, which is the use of food only as a means of sustenance, not for gratification of the taste buds. She is drawn to abhaya, that is absence of fear of anything, including physical harm or death. Her example indicates that human wants can be limited, basic needs met, and the spirit nurtured. Humanity can still choose a saner way of life, stepping lightly upon the earth, caring for all its creatures, living each day with contentment and harmony.

Gandhi understood truth as the basis of life. Truth and ahimsa were his guiding principles. Truth sustains the universe. Human beings ought to be ready to sacrifice anything, even laying down their lives if required, for upholding the truth. Describing ahimsa as identical with love, Gandhi advised us to love even our 'enemies'. If non-violence is the means, Truth is the end.

According to some scholars, several struggles in Manipur, including the two Nupilans, have been marked by satyagraha and non-cooperation.[51]

Irom Sharmila's epic fast—already the longest fast in human history, a fourteen-year long saga—is a non-violent act meant to achieve God-ordained goals. Nobody, least of all Sharmila, knows how much longer it is to carry on.

An indefinite fast, like most non-violent resistance, can be misconstrued as passive. People sometimes remark that rather than 'languish' in jail, she should give up her fast, come out and join the 'active struggle for change'.

One recalls the Gandhian claim that non-violence is an active force, not passive—active even when we sleep—for it works through the human heart. It is the law of humanity, just as violence is the law of the brute. 'An eye for an eye' might seem like a more active stand, being conspicuous and visible. Yet violence is hardly effective when the goal is to end abuse and injustice. Violence breeds violence. Revenge creates conditions for counter-revenge, not for justice or peace.

Non-violence is a weapon of the strong. It implies an ethical choice, balanced against expediency. Most practitioners of non-violence could access other means, including brute force. Yet they consciously reject the option, and strive to achieve non-violence, a perfection involving great discipline. They work constantly on two essential fronts, the inner and the outer. Fasting, as a means of non-violent intervention, has a psychological impact, affecting the opponents' activities and the operation of their systems.

Irom Sharmila has resolved that, come what may, she will not give up her fast until AFSPA is repealed. At points she has expressed a desire to marry, and have children, yet reiterated she will do as only after AFSPA is withdrawn. Her actions express willpower, not helplessness or absence of choice. She could well have picked up weapons, stepped across to join the ranks of insurgents. Their goals, after all, seem to overlap. Insurgents too demand an end to state violence and injustice. They want AFSPA repealed, and appropriate developmental policies put in place. But the methods through which they try to achieve their ends include extortion, injury, guns and bombs. According to non-violent practitioners like Sharmila, ignoble means cannot achieve noble ends.

Through her 'long fast' she intends to bring about an end to human violence. It is to be a voluntary end, achieved through a change of heart, a conversion of beliefs. In a world hurtling towards self-destruction, she is a quiet revolutionary, a radical who, by taking one giant step, is blazing a new trail. Through her determined fast, she is making a thousand different statements, all showing the way to a very different, ethically founded, just and humane world.

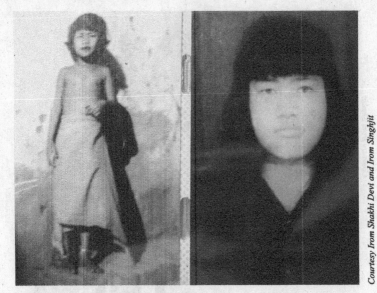

Irom Sharmila as a child; and a schoolgirl.

Sharmila (second from right), a young woman, with friends.

Sharmila,
pillion-riding.

Sharmila's mother
Irom Shakhi Devi.

Sharmila's father Irom
Nanda Singh.

Sharmila's grandmother Irom Tonsija Devi, aged 104 on 23 April 2007. By her side a tem—long wooden weaving tool, also used as a weapon of defence.

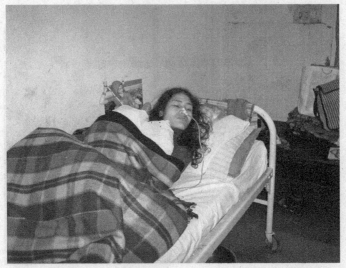

Irom Sharmila in Ram Manohar Lohia Hospital, New Delhi, 2 March 2007. Beside her is a statue of Meerabai, gifted by a nurse.

Irom Sharmila in the Security Ward of Jawaharlal
Nehru Hospital, Imphal, with the author.

Ima Mangol Devi, an active Meira Paibi leader in conversation
with Irom Singhjit, Sharmila's elder brother.

A demonstration by the Meira Paibis to repeal APSPA in the 1980s.

A Meira Paibi delegation—lobbying with government and army top brass, 1980s.

Ima Taruni Devi (left) and Ima Ramani Devi (right), senior Meira Paibi leaders. Along with some other activists, they live and work in the small All Manipur Women's Social Reformation and Development Samaj office, having dedicated their lives to the cause.

The Nupilan Memorial commemorates Manipuri women's brave struggles against colonial exploitation during the Second Nupilan, 1939.

Ten Innocents Memorial Park, at Malom village, commemorates the ten persons killed by security forces on 2 November 2000. Irom Sharmila began her fast in protest against the massacre, on 5 November 2000.

Govindjee Temple, in Kangla Fort. The government opened Kangla Fort to the public on 20 November 2004.

Lai Haraoba, the ancient dance, led by Maibis, priestesses.
Lai Haraoba ritually enacts the creation of the universe, of human beings,
and activities like weaving and house-building.

Khwairamband Bazar in Imphal, reputed to be the largest women's
market in Asia. Women vendors start bringing their wares at 4 a.m.;
the market continues late into the night, when, in the absence of
electricity, it is lit by candles and lanterns.

CIVIL DISOBEDIENCE AND DEMOCRATIC DISSENT

'One person who can express ahimsa in life exercises a force superior to all the forces of brutality.'

—M.K. Gandhi[52]

During the 1990s, Irom Sharmila took part in conventional forms of protest—petitions and memoranda, demonstrations and commissions. But she found that none of these was effective in putting an end to rampant violence in her state. State-inflicted violence was stoking the fires of insurgency, until a macabre dance of death stalked the land. People's democratic protests had not affected the approach of the state. When all else seemed insufficient, Irom Sharmila chose to break the law by fasting indefinitely. Her protest is directed at the unjust law that renders state brutality 'lawful'.

Irom Sharmila is a law-abiding citizen—as were Gandhi, Thoreau, Martin Luther King and Rosa Parks. King, a priest and activist deeply sensitive to social ills, adopted non-violence as a way to change societal structures. Parks broke the law simply by sitting in a public bus in Alabama, in a seat reserved for whites. Parks was arrested, and this became an issue around which opinion crystallized contributing to the groundswell of

113

the American Civil Rights Movement of the '60s and '70s. The struggle drew world attention and sympathy to the anti-racist cause, and gradually the laws and thinking changed.

Many decades before these events, in the early years of the twentieth century Gandhi had sent a flood of petitions and memoranda to persuade authorities to change blatantly racist legislation in South Africa. Later, after returning to India, he took similar action in the context of the exploitative colonial regime. But in each instance, the authorities remained unmoved. After much reflection and deliberation, he decided he had little option but to break the law. Submitting to injustice was intolerable to his sensibility, and other methods were proving ineffective. On several occasions, therefore, he went ahead and broke the law, for instance, producing salt, although it was banned by the British authorities. He demanded just laws, respecting people's basic entitlements and rights.

Like Gandhi, Irom Sharmila reposes faith in democracy based on just laws. Democracy is precious: and it needs to be strengthened through people's active participation. In India's present-day parliamentary democracy, there exists a yawning abyss between common citizens and their elected 'representatives'. Many politicians are power-hungry, opportunistic and corrupt. The state protects the interests of the wealthy, of global conglomerates, often at the expense of the deprived and dispossessed. Corporate interests run on the logic of profit, not equity or ethics. Public provision of health, education and welfare services, though significant, is highly inadequate. The socio-economic scenario is marked by widening disparities; extreme poverty, unemployment and hunger are daily realities for millions.

At the same time, India has a vibrant public sphere, with people of different persuasions putting forward their views. The fact that millions of people are marginalized fuels diverse people's movements—on issues such as displacement due to gigantic dam projects and SEZs, trawlers that destroy fisher people's livelihoods, farmers' suicides due to pauperization and indebtedness, and denial of minimum wages to mineworkers. People are struggling for the right to information, right to food, right to education, right to livelihood, and even—in areas where armed forces have been granted 'special' powers—the right to life.

The laws granting special powers to armed forces have been promulgated by government with the stated intention of *protecting* citizens and maintaining internal security. Yet innumerable armed forces personnel—military and paramilitary—have dishonoured their uniform by killing unarmed, innocent people in false encounters, in Jammu and Kashmir, Manipur, Chhattisgarh, Jharkhand and elsewhere. Even one reported crime of this magnitude ought to be thoroughly investigated in a democracy, but we have thousands such, with no redress. As a corollary to this situation, those fighting for human rights and those documenting cases of state violation of human rights, are being arrested. Binayak Sen and Irom Sharmila are among the best known of these: both jailed by the state. Sen, a public health specialist devoted to working with tribal communities, and national vice-president of the People's Union for Civil Liberties (PUCL), was jailed for nearly three years, on trumped-up charges of sedition; until the Supreme Court ordered his release (May 2011).

To a state guilty of allowing impunity to its own forces, demands for transparency and honouring of human rights can appear as a threat. Human rights defenders challenge the legitimacy of a state which is allowing violations by its own armed forces. They urge the state to adopt democratic means of resolving conflicts. Nowhere in the country have 'special' laws managed to curb terrorism or insurgency. But, for the Indian state, the meaning of 'threat to internal security' seems to have shifted and changed, becoming the exact opposite of the original intent: the 'people' the state is supposed to defend are now perceived as the 'threat' that it actually extinguishes.

In an era where untruth masquerades as truth, the powerful feel threatened by those who speak with the voice of conscience.

Satyagraha, non-cooperation and civil disobedience are based on the logic that if rulers are unjust, citizenry can—and in fact, should—refuse to cooperate with them. People must obey their conscience, and if the laws of the land are contrary to the dictates of their conscience, they are justified in defying those laws. While satyagraha implies resistance to injustice by the force of truth, and non-cooperation is refusal to fit into an unjust system, civil disobedience goes further: it is the active and open defiance of unjust state laws.

Some critics question the need to practise civil disobedience in a democracy. But in fact, civil disobedience comes into play after authorities fail to respond to people's appeals, petitions and memoranda. Involving principled resistance to the wrongdoing of those in power, it spurs on the process of democratization. It is integral to the process of fully establishing and upholding a democracy. If the polity is host to many evils, civil disobedience can, and *should*, be practised to expose these evils. Individual conscience should guide its need. So long as practitioners of civil disobedience are non-violent, and willing to pay the penalty when they violate an unjust law, they are abiding by the country's Constitution. Their violation of the law is specific, limited, and deliberate. It is designed to achieve a higher aim: significant improvements in laws, policies and politics of the nation.

ॐ

Irom Sharmila is a practitioner of non-cooperation and, indeed, civil disobedience, for according to the state she is openly breaking one law, even as she protests for the withdrawal of another law. By refusing to eat, following the dictates of her conscience, she has been labelled an outlaw. While the authorities treat her fast as an infringement of law, she points out that AFSPA is infringing a higher law.

Thoreau, pioneering theorist of civil disobedience, advised people to disobey unjust laws. By so doing, conscientious objectors expose such laws to public scrutiny. They reveal the inherent brutality of these laws, and the anti-people aspect of the ruling dispensation that imposes them. Thoreau saw principled resistance as a duty of the righteous citizen: 'Under a government which imprisons any unjustly, the true place for a just man is also in prison.'[53] Thoreau and Tolstoy advocated civil disobedience to vindicate the right to pursue one's individual conscience.

Socrates violated the law when he taught young people to think for themselves, and ask questions. He maintained it was his right to ask questions and voice dissent. The state arrested, jailed, and sentenced him to death. Although associates urged him to escape, he accepted the punishment meted out, drinking the cup of hemlock with equanimity. He died, yet his voice was not silenced. His pupil Plato spread his teachings; in the

Platonic dialogues, Socrates argues that although he seems to break the law, in reality he is obeying a higher law, that of his conscience. A good Constitution must respect this. He accepts punishment cheerfully, and claims, through all this, to be a patriotic, even model, citizen.

Aung San Suu Kyi speaks of fearlessness, and the 'supremacy of moral force over force based on the might of arms and empire'.[54] The military regime in Myanmar placed Suu Kyi under house arrest in 1989 for making pro-democracy speeches. Although Suu Kyi's party the National League for Democracy (NLD) won a landslide victory in national elections in 1990, the regime refused to recognize this, and she continued to survive house arrest, for virtually twenty-one years. She was briefly released a few times, but soon re-arrested. Pro-democracy colleagues and supporters were attacked, jailed and killed. Resistance was suppressed, yet erupted intermittently. For instance in September 2007, over 100,000 people engaged in peaceful protests, on the streets of Yangon and other cities of Myanmar. The junta cracked down on protestors, including monks and lay activists. Worldwide, governments spoke out, asking Myanmar to be responsive to its people, and democratize its institutions. The UN made efforts to mediate and set afoot a peace process in Myanmar. Aung San Suu Kyi became the conscience of her nation, and an icon for democratic movements around the world.

In November 2010 general elections were held in Myanmar and Suu Kyi was released from house arrest, The world celebrated her release. Like with Irom Sharmila, Suu Kyi's fearlessness and resolute commitment, despite physical isolation, have been remarkable, and widely respected.

There is much in common between the struggles waged by these two women. Both seemingly delicate and frail human beings are untiring in their resistance. Even when detained by government, each indomitable woman wielded moral and emotional influence.. Both 'iron ladies' are feared by their national governments, for they have the potential to mobilize wide support, and the powers-that-be live in dread of their popularity. In struggling non-violently against state violence, and sacrificing normal life for peace, each has become an icon, an ideal and an inspiration. Suu Kyi and Irom Sharmila have both suffered harsh deprivation, and denial of basic freedom, yet they have refused to back out. Their strength lies in their rock-like determination, and the resonance and near-reverence this arouses in others. They remind us of our common humanity. They suffer, we feel, for all of us: and we are humbled, and inspired, by that realization.

Social progress has always depended on those who do not hesitate to break existing laws, whether religious, social or political, as part of a calculated drive towards evolution of better laws. Their contributions are essential for the wider good. Most national freedom fighters broke the law at one point or another. They accepted the obligation to bear witness to the truth, and suffered the consequences.

Soul-force, pitted against brute force: stark polarities confront world citizens today. While most sensitive people intuitively respect soul-force and abhor brute force, often they remain silent. They live in the shadow of fear, for the opponents are invariably vengeful, and often ruthless. People go about their daily business quietly, not speaking their minds, lest they should be suspected of criticizing the state, or worse—siding with the insurgents. Many ordinary citizens internalize the logic of the state, and defend it even when it is unjust, or violent. They feel a sense of false security when men in uniform enforce 'law and order', though they are aware that the same forces engineer false encounters, and repeated acts of violence against innocents. Thus when some people speak out against the violence, a silent public offers strong support. When they see a person bravely resisting state violence, ready to face any consequences, they are stirred by the power of non-violence.

Questions crowd into our minds. Can soul-force win? Is not 'turning the other cheek' an indication of powerlessness? Will people voluntarily let go of the privileges of power? Can power be exercised without corruption? Many people have died for freedom and for peace—have their sacrifices been in vain? Is any of this—sticking to one's ideals, refusing to cow down, listening to and acting upon one's conscience—effective? Or is the suffering, undertaken voluntarily, in vain? Should we, on the other hand, stand by while cruelty reigns and the world is daily destroyed? Can we allow a callous system to rule and control our world? Can we let innocents be slaughtered? Will the human spirit accept defeat at the hands of orchestrated power? How can the potential of civil society to act for peace be effectively channelized?

While the answers are not easy, Irom Sharmila's action provides significant pointers. As with Gandhi, she too is clear that the right ends cannot be attained by the wrong means.

Her example is instructive. Rather than lament, criticize and despair, she has taken up the good fight in her own quiet, firm way. Practising non-violence as a way of life, she has linked it to socio-political goals that affect wider humanity. For her, non-violence is not simply a tool; rather, it is a fundamental principle of life, inextricably bound up with her basic values. Her attitude reminds us that non-violence is akin to love, in the sense of deep compassion and fellow feeling for all beings. Although its workings are partly invisible, clearly it is a powerful and active force. Like every other satyagrahi, Sharmila looks upon everybody, even the opponent in a particular situation, as basically a friend. Non-violence is not a weapon of the weak, but of 'the stoutest hearts'.[55]

Multiple crises loom large in India, more than sixty-seven years after independence. Gandhi is frequently invoked, a forgotten messiah whom we reclaim sporadically, having neglected him to our peril. His thoughts illuminate the possibility of another kind of politics. Many versions of his philosophy are flourishing, including Gandhigiri, inspired by a popular film in which the quirky hero offers flowers to his opponents rather than throwing brickbats. Irom Sharmila's version goes far beyond, its challenge more thoroughgoing. Non-violence is an exacting discipline: a spiritual force applied to all departments of life—personal, social and political; local, national and international. A single individual can, through this spiritual discipline, challenge the unjust might of an empire.

Irom Sharmila has become a spokesperson for peace in Manipur, her homeland. At the same time, she speaks for all human beings. Her struggle is a nucleus around which civil rights and pro-democracy forces gather. An invincible spirit, strong will and sharp intelligence are her weapons, as well as love, compassion and empathy.

She is young, yet living almost as an ascetic. She has become known as a symbol of peace; but she is neither a mere symbol nor is she only spirit. While in jail, she exchanged letters and grew close to somebody, whom she has said she would like to marry one day. She is a vitally alive human being, enduring solitary confinement every moment, year after year. Nothing exemplifies her principles more than the courageous acceptance of incarceration, the uncomplaining endurance of imposed hardship and cruel suffering. Kept away from family, friends and colleagues, she meets only Home Guards, police personnel and nurses, day after day. Apart from these agents of the state that has made her captive, she lives by herself, alone.

She chooses to express dissent, and submit to the punishment meted out. State forces arrest her, but cannot compel her to change her thinking, apologize or retreat. The indefinite protest has made her a living challenge.

After years of imprisonment in Chinese jails, a number of Tibetan Buddhists have emerged, seemingly unscathed. They explain that, when kept in solitude, they meditated, using the space to practise mindfulness and develop inner qualities, rather than squander time in useless complaint, anger and bitterness. Jailers were able to lock up these political dissenters, but could not crush their spirit of resistance, nor break their resolve to carry on speaking and fighting for freedom. For Irom Sharmila too, in a way the jail hospital has become her monastery or her ashram: a place to develop qualities of endurance, patience, fearlessness and inner confidence. At the same time, she longs and waits for the day when, the mission achieved, she can walk free, and live as she wants.

WIDENING CIRCLES: FLIGHT TO DELHI

Irom Sharmila has been subjected to an endless pattern of judicial custody, release, and re-arrest. On 2 February 2006, the procedure was repeated. She was released, and re-arrested on the same day. She was then in the sixth year of her indefinite fast. On 16 February she was produced before the magistrate and sent to judicial custody. She was kept once again in the Security Ward of JN Hospital, Imphal.

She bore her isolation with stoic calm, immersing herself in yoga and reading, but there were deliberate attempts to harass her, cruelly adding to her discomfort. Security guards, who stayed in the hospital, took to cooking their meals in her room: a deliberate attempt to torture a person who had long ago given up the taste and smell of food. On 26 July 2006 her counsel filed a curious application: seeking a direction to shift the cooking of food by lady security guards away from Sharmila's hospital room. The court directed jail authorities to shift the cooking away from her room with immediate effect.

On 29 September, her counsel filed an application for Sharmila's unconditional release. On 3 October 2006, the court released her from custody.

This time, Irom Sharmila decided to break out of the routine. She knew the police would re-arrest her very soon, if she continued her fast within the territory of Manipur. In the interim, she was a free bird. She exercised her freedom by leaving Manipur and flying to Delhi. This was a well-thought-out move, planned quietly, in conjuction with her brother Singhjit, and a couple of activist colleagues, Babloo Loitongbam of HRA, and student leader Sapamcha Kangleipal. Her intention was to spread news of her campaign, further and wider. It was important to reach out to the rest of the world.

On 4 October 2006, Sharmila left for Delhi. As she puts it, 'From Manipur I escaped to Delhi. Here it is international. I can get attention for the cause from many more people. Manipur is only one state; that also other people do not know anything about.'

She fully expected to be intercepted at Imphal airport. In fact Singhjit did not carry any clothes—he did not think Sharmila would actually be allowed past the security check. They had bought her ticket under the name 'I.S. Chanu',* which may have helped conceal her identity. A Union minister was travelling by the same flight, so airport security clustered around him. However, as human rights activist Rita Manchanda opines, airport functionaries would almost certainly have recognized Irom Sharmila; it is after all a tiny airport, and she a very well-known figure. Perhaps they deliberately turned a blind eye, secretly sympathetic to her cause!

After years in jail, virtually in solitary confinement, Sharmila was free! She hoped to evade the vicious cycle of arrests and

---

*Chanu is an honorific, commonly attached to the name of a single woman: thus, 'Irom Sharmila Chanu'

re-arrests, and reach out with her message to many diverse people. The flight inspired her to write (in Meiteilon):

Beyond This Tangled Visible World

Beyond this tangled visible world
I flew to heaven in an airplane
Reaching That Land
Where my Maker was to test me
Enchanted, but also fearful,
Taking the shape of a cloud,
I find myself eye to eye with the gods

What an awesome form it is
That vibration in the void,
How joyful, how electrifying
I marvel in awe as I remember,
Beyond the illusions of this world

In that land of harmonious life,
There is no space for the body
What are eyes and ears?
What after all are hands and feet?

Hearing there is no essential difference
Between divine form and human,
I knew not how different they are
How are we to compare—
This world and that
Place with no birth, no death,
How express that wonder?

I express what I know
The sightless shall see

Those without hearing will hear
Of cosmic creation, human emotion and
Supreme knowledge of That Essence
Space is filled with its vibrations

Those people are without delusions
No high and low, all are equal there
They feel no jealousy like worldly folks
There is no despair or dissatisfaction
I can hardly explain—
They have no profit or loss there

Freely they move in their duties,
Enveloped by soft, strong light
Nothing is impossible or unreachable
In that place where truth is lucid and pure
No excuse exists for untruth
Human wrongs are punished
Not excused or ignored.[56]

Sharmila was deeply occupied, as she came 'eye to eye with the gods', with the cosmic nature of her struggle. She had a vision of a heavenly world, principled and pure, where truth and justice prevail. She perceived the inherent possibility of harmonious life, which she seeks to actualize through her non-violent protest.

She confirmed her commitments as soon as she arrived at Palam Airport, New Delhi. She left the airport for Rajghat, Mahatma Gandhi's samadhi. She went there to pay homage to his spirit. The green, open memorial soothed her, offering her a rare moment of peace and communion.

She placed a wreath of flowers at his samadhi, and sat in prayer. Word about her arrival in Delhi spread like wildfire among human rights activists. Rojesh recalls, 'I had no idea she would be coming to Delhi. Obviously it was kept a secret. My friend from Jamia Millia University called me saying, "Come to Rajghat, Sharmila Didi is there." I could not believe it at first. I said, "Sharmila Didi in Delhi? It can't be!" I immediately went to Rajghat, and found her there.'

Journalists got wind of her arrival, and rushed to Rajghat. After placing marigolds on Gandhi's samadhi and joining her palms in silent prayer, Sharmila sat on the soft grass in a pensive mood. A white shawl draped over her curly black hair, she replied thoughtfully to journalists' queries. She noted the Indian government was betraying Gandhi's memory in its treatment of the people of Manipur, and its reaction to her peaceful protest.

From Rajghat the small knot of activists and media persons repaired to Jantar Mantar, the city's chief spot for political protests. A potpourri of issues is often raised here, by dissenters from different parts of this vast country. Sundry protests attract no more than the faintly curious attention of passers-by, who rush to and from work or market. A few months before Irom Sharmila's arrival at Jantar Mantar, leaders of Narmada Bachao Andolan (NBA), the world's foremost anti-dam movement, sat here on hunger strike. The media visited Jantar Mantar then, especially when Medha Patkar and two other village activists of the NBA went on hunger strike. Across the road sat survivors of the world's worst industrial disaster, the Bhopal Gas Tragedy of 1984. Posters and banners with slogans expressing issues and demands, through colour and cartoon, lined both sides of Parliament Street.

When Irom Sharmila arrived at Jantar Mantar, it was a

relatively quiet day. The tiny contingent of Manipuri activists parked itself on the pavement opposite Jantar Mantar, the centuries-old observatory whose curling walls, strange clocks and cosmic markers spiral into the sky, tracking the movements of stars and the sun. To the left a road leads to cosmopolitan YMCA and the majestic beauty of Rakabganj Gurdwara. Surrealistic, yet without dissonance, the glass and concrete skyscrapers of a modern metropolis are visible in Connaught Place, the bustling business hub, a stone's throw away.

Sharmila settled down at this hallowed spot. The weary traveller, who began her day early at the high-security Imphal airport, had journeyed to New Delhi, and arrived at her destination in the pulsating nerve centre of the city—indeed, of the country. She slept, curled on a rug, while supporters hoisted a shamiana to shelter the protesters. She renewed her energies only through sleep, while others ate.

People gathered around the fasting protester: students, members of human rights groups, women's organizations and ordinary citizens. Rugs were spread out for everybody to sit on, converted into makeshift beds by night. By evening, Sharmila had to use a blanket, for there was a nip in the air. Students put up impromptu banners and posters to inform passers-by about AFSPA. Newspapers, next morning, reported Irom Sharmila's arrival in the capital. The chief minister of Manipur, K. Ibobi Singh, happened to be in New Delhi for a meeting. He came to Jantar Mantar, and tried to persuade Sharmila to call off her fast. True to character, she refused.

Her move to Delhi drew immediate international attention. Reuters reported on 4 October 2006: 'An Indian woman who has been on hunger strike for six years against human rights abuses in the remote northeastern state of Manipur

shifted her fight to the capital New Delhi on Wednesday ...'
Sharmila was happy at the attention her cause was receiving.
But by 5 October, her physical energy was fading, since she
had consumed nothing, not even a drop of water, since release
from jail on 3 October.

Around midnight of 5–6 October, Parliament Street police
swooped down on the bunch of activists. Supporters, including
several Delhi students and women's rights activists, were
ordered into a police van, while Sharmila was whisked away
in a police jeep. Soon after the jeep drove away with her, the
rest were released. She was taken to the All India Institute
of Medical Science (AIIMS) in south Delhi, and placed in
Ward No. 57, New Private Wards.

On 11 October 2006, human rights groups, with students
and activist supporters, held a mass demonstration demanding
immediate repeal of AFSPA.

Advocate Colin Gonsalves, of the Human Rights Law
Network, helped Irom Singhjit to file a habeas corpus petition
demanding that his sister be produced in court and charges
against her spelt out. She was not even shown a copy of the
FIR on the basis of which she was picked up, despite repeated
requests: a flagrant violation of basic procedure.

On 13 November, AIIMS issued a discharge slip to Sharmila.
But the police would not allow her to move. Sharmila refused
nasal feeding in protest against her arbitrary detention, and
the indignity of her position. AIIMS authorities agreed to
keep her, but remained hostile. They were already stressed
out, with many doctors sitting on strike against the newly
announced caste-based reservations policy!

A large number of people visited Sharmila. She found the
police guards easy-going, compared to the Home Guards

back in Imphal. She was, in any case, not under arrest: the police said she was in 'preventive detention', and 'free to go if the doctors allow her'. Police and government seemed confused: they did not want to let her die, since that would attract international criticism, but they were not keen to arrest her either. They brought her into hospital, force-fed her, and kept guard. Questions were raised in Parliament, and answered evasively, with vague promises about repealing the Act, and appeals to Sharmila to call off her fast. In early December, a home ministry official visited; no other government official deigned to even pay her a visit. The prime minister and the President of India did not reply to the letters she sent them.

Room No. 57, New Private Wards, became the gathering point for a motley group of activists. AIIMS being centrally located in the city facilitated access. A number of visitors dropped by daily, and the police allowed them in after a cursory registration. Policemen bore long rifles but were otherwise relaxed, since this was pleasant duty: all they had to do was sit outside the door of a harmless woman, who had gentle and polite visitors. If they were bored, they would open her room door, twirl the TV set round, and watch a film, serial or cricket match. This they could handle.

Sharmila was often alone in her ward. She spent the time reading, thinking or doing yogasanas, including the head-stand, shoulder-stand and exercises essential for her digestive system. She explained, 'I stay healthy by doing yogasanas. There is no fixed time. I can do it in the morning, some in the afternoon, more in the night. It is very, very important for me ... If I do not do yoga I will become ill.'

She observed, 'Here in Delhi they feed me milk with some

nutrient added to it. It is not fresh milk. It is powdered milk, out of a tin. They make it once in the day and put it in a big bottle. It is very expensive. They give me a laxative also. They feed me five or six times a day here. In Manipur they boiled rice, dal and vegetables, and fed me the liquid through the tube. I felt better with that. Here I have only milk, and it makes me feel ill.' The daily diet of milk upset her system, leading to diarrhoea and rapid weight loss. She refused to take in anything for a few days, growing weaker by the day.

Some NGOs in Imphal released a cassette of Irom Sharmila's poems, sung by well-known singers. A friend brought one copy of the cassette from Imphal to Delhi, for Sharmila. She was delighted, and showed it to the nurse, who unfortunately took it away. 'She thought it was a gift and kept it. I asked her, "It is in my mother tongue. How will you understand it?" She said, "I will ask somebody to translate it for me. There are many nurses from Manipur in this hospital."'

On 26 November 2006, Nobel Laureate Shirin Ebadi visited her in hospital. The Iranian peace activist issued statements urging the Indian government to revoke the law giving sweeping powers to security forces. She expressed her solidarity and support to the Manipuri cause. The press reported that Ebadi planned to take up the matter with the UN High Commissioner on Human Rights, and the UN Human Rights Council. She said she was deeply moved and touched by the non-violent and long struggle of Sharmila. She added that the army was for people's protection, and should never be used against them.

Sharmila enjoyed having visitors. 'I do not like to watch TV,' she said, 'I have no interest in it. I can find any situation valuable. Here just now, this situation in Delhi is very valuable.

I am learning a lot from being in this situation. So many people come to meet me.'

Her tiny ward soon filled up with books. When people realized she liked to read, they would bring an offering, something she might want to peruse. She asked her brother Singhjit, and a few trusted friends, to get particular books for her.

The India Social Forum (ISF), held in New Delhi in December 2006, requested Irom Sharmila to make the keynote address at its opening. The police would not permit her to go, although the venue was just a few minutes from AIIMS. She sent her keynote address, a brief message of solidarity which was read out to the gathering of thousands of people. Participating in ISF were movements representing the voices and aspirations of millions of people from various parts of the world, committed to creating an alternative globalization, based on different, people-oriented models. Several of them visited Sharmila in her hospital ward.[57]

During ISF, a panel discussion was held on 'Political Movements and the Nationality Question in North-east India', organized by Manipur Research Forum, Delhi. Dr Bhagat Oinam of Jawaharlal Nehru University highlighted the need to understand issues of territoriality in any claims made by the nation state, and by other stakeholders. Noni Meetei highlighted the importance of historical experience in understanding nationalist movements in the North-East. Journalist Kazu Ahmed pointed out that minority communities were often alienated in nationalist movements, as happened with Bodos, Miris, Dimashas and Muslims in Assam. Joyson Mazamo of Naga Peoples' Movement for Human Rights outlined manipulative tactics used by the Indian state towards dissenting voices, including the ethnic Naga movement. Researcher Bimol Akoijam stressed on the need to network between diverse voices of the marginalized. All present agreed on the importance of dialogue between political movements in north-east India, to understand each other's political positions and possible sharing of spaces.

Meanwhile, Sharmila's supporters planned another public demonstration in December, protesting repressive policies in the North-East. The corridor outside Private Ward No. 57 became a busy makeshift office. Police guards, on lofty chairs, ignored the three or four men who camped on a rug on the cold floor. Onil K. keyed in invitations for the demonstration, using his laptop. Singhjit fell ill with a heavy cold and lay dozing, a newspaper spread over his face. A number of human rights activists, students and women's groups took part in the demonstration.

On 12 December, Indian Parliament appealed to Irom Sharmila to end her indefinite fast. 'We all appeal to Irom Sharmila to call off her fast,' Somnath Chatterjee, Lok Sabha Speaker, said. P.A. Sangma, of the ruling party, raised the matter, drawing the attention of the House to Ms Sharmila's 'critical' condition. Sharmila's response to the appeal was characteristic. Quietly and calmly, she reiterated her consistent stand: she would eat the moment AFSPA is removed from Manipur, not before.

On 18 December 2006, the police suddenly removed Irom Sharmila, again at the dead of night, from AIIMS to Ram Manohar Lohia Hospital (RMLH). They did not give any prior intimation, so much so that brother Singhjit, who normally slept in the corridor outside her room, missed the departure because he had stepped out for a few minutes.

He made frantic enquiries, and then hired a three-wheeler to take him to RMLH. Subsequent visitors were shocked to find an empty room. When I went to pay her a visit on 20 December, and could not find her, I went around making inquiries from nurses and the hospital administration. But the AIIMS personnel were tight-lipped and would not reveal Sharmila's whereabouts.

At RMLH, Sharmila was kept in Room No. 8A, New Private Wards, a smaller room than at AIIMS, but even more convenient for the police, since it had a tiny annexe, wherein they made themselves comfortable. Her brother too slept in this annexe, rather than the corridor: a blessing, considering it was by now a bitterly cold winter. Friends and colleagues hovered around. Among the regulars were lawyer Preeti Verma, feminist activist Vani Subramaniam, research scholars Onil K. and Thoiba from Delhi University's History Department, journalist Kullajit, publisher Meera Johri, dancer Charu Shankar, Kaushalji the elderly Gandhian, and a smiling young Sikh couple with their small child. For me, visiting Sharmila was like homecoming—a warm welcome always assured.

Sharmila, at the centre of it all, read endlessly, voraciously—books on religion, revolution, folk tales and literature. She went through Greek mythology, Japanese folk tales, and Che Guevara's *Motorcycle Diaries*. She read the lives of Himalayan mystics. She devoured Manipuri poetry, classics, and daily newspapers. One day she said, 'I am reading the Upanishads, Buddhism, Quran and Bible. I am interested in all the religions.' She added wistfully, 'My English is not good. My brother knows English and Hindi. His English is also not good.'

She would walk in the small garden near her ward, musing. I accompanied her sometimes. She keenly observed trees, plants, birds and squirrels, asking detailed questions, plumbing the depths of my knowledge until I ran out of answers. She said, 'I learn everything from nature. Everything we make is based on nature. We must observe nature, and see what is there. An aeroplane, if you see, is just like a mosquito. See its wings, how it moves ...' Much of her inner strength derives from the rhythms and wisdom of the natural order. She spoke of death. Death is a part of nature, and she takes it as such, in her stride. Just as she was born, in accordance with a higher design, so she will one day die, for it is essential to the natural order of things.

One day when I reached RMLH, Sharmila was doing the head-stand—her tall frame motionless, upside down for a good ten minutes, while I waited. The policewoman explained, with enormous respect, that this is a daily occurrence. She added, her khakhi uniform oddly discordant with her sentiments, 'Ye to mahatma hain.' (She is a great spirit, a great person.)

The nurse, who fed milk to Sharmila through the nasal tube, gifted her one day with a statue of Meerabai, the medieval mystic singer-poet. Sharmila treasured the statue, keeping it next to her pillow, and taking it with her when she returned to Imphal. Perhaps she felt a kinship with that creative, independent-minded woman, a poet like herself.

Another policewoman confided one day, 'I studied Hindi in college. I always loved poetry, and this lady reminds me of Meerabai.' Certainly there is a resemblance between freedom-loving Meera, who renounced her palace and stepped out onto the streets, singing and dancing, and Sharmila, who has given up home and hearth, seeking justice and freedom for her people.

Meanwhile, the RMLH administration and doctors arbitrarily denied access to visitors. A college student from Miranda House, who wished to write an article about Irom Sharmila as an inspiring youth icon, was made to wait for half a day, and then flatly denied permission to meet Sharmila. In fact, there was no legitimate ground for such denial, nor was it imposed consistently. Had the student known which ward Sharmila was lodged in, she could have gone there directly, and nobody would have stopped her. Clearly there were cross-currents at work, and some malicious intent.

Students from Lady Shri Ram College, who went to meet Sharmila in January 2007, went straight to her ward. Twenty-three young women stuffed into her tiny room and spent a precious half-hour chatting with Sharmila, asking her about her family, her politics, the fast, her favourite colours ... They were charmed, and deeply respectful. The nurse, who came on a routine round, was shocked to find such an abundance of visitors, and threw them out at once. The police were relatively easy-going: the maximum work they ever did was to comb through a bouquet of flowers brought by some visitor, in search for bombs. 'Don't you know the bomb that killed Rajiv Gandhi was brought in a bouquet of flowers?' they queried belligerently, convinced they were protecting the gentle lady from harm.

By February 2007, Irom Sharmila grew restive, and considered returning to Imphal. The national media had lost interest in her, after a spate of articles during the initial weeks. RMLH is tucked away in one corner of Delhi, making it less accessible for journalists and other visitors. Sharmila felt she would be more useful, now, in Manipur. Elections were coming up there, and her presence was likely to make a difference. Some younger friends suggested she travel elsewhere, like Geneva, to garner support for the cause, but she disagreed, insisting that her place was back in Manipur. She applied for permission to return home.

The home ministry asked doctors to certify whether she was healthy enough to travel. A medical check-up was conducted, and reports came in showing she was fit. 'Then suddenly,' recalls Singhjit, 'a new medical superintendent came and gave a new report. His report said she was not fit to travel.' The Congress party in Manipur, which was the ruling party at the Centre as well, evidently did not want Irom Sharmila to return to Manipur. Her return was likely to influence the electorate, swaying voter sympathy towards smaller parties like the Manipur People's Party, which were championing the anti-AFSPA cause.

Agitated and unhappy about her forced detention in Delhi, she fretted and fumed: 'I have no power. The government has control over me. I cannot go anywhere. I cannot go to my home state. They decide.' She registered her protest against this new indignity, by refusing nasal feeding. Over the next few days, her condition again deteriorated.

Immediately after the elections in Manipur in late February, RMLH doctors declared Irom Sharmila was fit to travel, and the home ministry gave her permission to return to Manipur.

Just before her departure, the police filed a charge sheet against her, and immediately granted bail. This was on 3 March 2007. She remained in RMLH while Singhjit, accompanied by lawyer and an activist friends, went to the police station and completed the legal work. She was to leave the next day.

The evening before her departure, Sharmila was sad as she bid goodbye to some of her closest friends in Delhi. 'Do not say goodbye,' she exclaimed, 'There is no goodbye between friends. We are together. We shall meet again.' Singhjit, ever the devoted brother, packed their bags—'Books, books, books,' he lamented. 'Two bags we have, both full of books only!' He was delighted to be returning to Imphal. His wife Shanti kept the household running by weaving and selling cloth, but it was not easy. Shanti supports Sharmila's cause, so much so that she saved bits of money from her weaving, and sent it to Delhi, to help them out. Their daughter was soon to sit for college exams, and elder son for school exams, so Singhjit was glad to go home, where he was much needed.

For Sharmila, returning to Manipur meant almost certain solitary confinement. Normally a calm presence, without warning that evening, she burst into tears. Brother Singhjit, brave co-warrior, found his powers of comprehension sorely tested: 'No reason,' he told us. 'There is no reason for her crying.' Her friends, there to take care of last-minute legalities and logistics and bid Sharmila farewell, were bewildered too, and a little at a loss. Yet deep down each one understood: she was a human being with strengths and weaknesses, a little vulnerable and forlorn, even though she was a 'mahatma'!

The next morning at 5 a.m., Irom Sharmila flew to Imphal, after five eventful months in Delhi. She journeyed with the moon, which went into eclipse at 3, and emerged by 6— luminous, silvery and full. She saw the moon emerge gradually from dark shadows, and illuminate the sky with its silver rays.

The very same day, 4 March 2007, within a few hours of

her arrival, while people across the country celebrated the festival of Holi, police picked her up and whisked her away. She was back in familiar terrain!

Her brother Irom Singhjit and human rights colleague Babloo Loitongbam were picked up, and released within a few hours. She, however, was isolated, charge-sheeted and, on 7 March 2007, remanded to judicial custody.

Perhaps she too is in eclipse. Surely, one day she will return to full freedom, the blight of AFSPA removed, and shine with glorious health.

SOLITARY CONFINEMENT

It is 19 April 2007 and I am scheduled to meet Irom Sharmila in the Security Ward of Jawaharlal Nehru Hospital (JNIMS) Imphal. This is where prisoners of Sajiwa Central Jail are kept if they require medical attention. I have in hand a permission letter, signed by the joint secretary, home ministry, Manipur. But when we arrive at 9.45 that morning, the Home Guard refuses to open the metal shutters. We plead, but she keeps shaking her head, impassive.

Not every day does one try to enter a jail. When leaving for Manipur six weeks earlier, Irom Sharmila had said, 'There is no goodbye between friends.' She chose to return to her home state, knowing fully well she would be arrested and jailed.

She had explained, in response to my frank bewilderment, 'When I came from Manipur to Delhi, I had been alone for a long time, in solitary confinement. I was like a hollow bamboo. I was empty. In Delhi, I made many relationships. I feel full. In jail, I will remember, and I will write. I will write a very long poem of 1,000 lines. I will write about society, all the events I have observed and experienced. I will be by myself, locked up like a parrot in a cage. Like that parrot, I will forget what the green fields look like, and the blue sky. But I will not be sad. God is testing me. I must make myself pure. Human beings have so much dirt inside us—greed, hatred, anger ... It is not easy to purify oneself. I have to keep up my work.'

'You will continue your fast?'

Without a moment's hesitation she replied, 'I will continue my fast. I will not eat until the Act is removed.'

ༀ

Permission to meet her is not easily granted. Each application for a visit faces a highly cumbersome procedure. It can take upto a month, and involves applying to the joint secretary, home department, Government of Manipur; DGP (Prison), Central Jail, Manipur; and additional superintendent, Sajiwa Jail, Manipur. If the application gets due clearance from all these offices, an inspector accompanies the visitor to meet Irom Sharmila. Obviously, the government is determined to isolate her from all contact with the outside world, in the hope of weakening the struggle.

JN Hospital where she is interred is barely a kilometre from her home. Family members frequently pass by the hospital, for it is on the road they take to town. They long to meet Sharmila, and may cast a quick sideways glance in the direction of the hospital, but are forced to be content with a silent message and an equally silent prayer.

Being family members does not make it any easier to obtain permission. In fact they are probably discriminated against, as are other ordinary Manipuris. A local lawyer explains, 'It is more difficult for Manipuris to get permission, because all Manipuris are suspect in the eyes of the state. They think any of us may be insurgents.'

I was granted permission fairly quickly. Being non-Manipuri helped. Also, the presence of my daughter, and a friend of hers, provided a homely, innocuous touch. We employed strategy, too. Our application letter suggested that these two teenagers befriended Sharmila during her stay in Delhi, and, visiting Imphal for a holiday, wanted to meet their friend. The mother, being with them, would naturally accompany during the visit to Sharmila. Nowhere did our application mention I was writing a book on Irom Sharmila!

JN Hospital is a government hospital, the second largest public hospital in Manipur. Billboards on family planning, TB and antenatal care greet us on the approach road. There is no sign to suggest that the Security Wing, at one end of the long, low building, is any different from the rest of the hospital. As we walk up the gravel, lots of patients and patients' families stream through the main entrance of the building. This side, however, is deserted. At first glance, nothing seems out of the ordinary. The lady Home Guard, in loose kurta and pants, with close-cropped hair, is polite, but vigorously refuses to open the shutters to let us in. We hold the permission paper to her face, equally vigorous. She fetches another Home Guard to look at the paper, then both vanish.

After ten minutes they re-emerge and let us in, indicating we should sit on a wooden bench just inside the dark, dingy corridor. I see a small-built nurse scurry past, eyes lowered, cap stiff, coat and sari pure white. We catch a glimpse of half a dozen armed guards in deep blue uniforms, bearing heavy rifles, at the other end of the long corridor.

A senior superintendent saunters in. He informs us that we will have to get permission from the local police. We already have permission from the home ministry, which is well over and above the local police. But the authorities seem determined to make the procedure as long-winded as possible, logic or no logic. Sensing our apprehension and unease, the superintendent smiles, 'I will be here to welcome you.' This touch of kindness takes us by surprise.

At Porompat police station, Imphal East, the SP expresses intense irritation with Irom Sharmila and her supporters. He asks roughly, 'Why doesn't she take bail? Why don't you persuade her to take bail, and take her home?' Singhjit remains silent. The query is purely rhetorical, and everybody knows it. To take bail, Sharmila will have to swear that she will not repeat her 'crime', that is, she will have to call off her hunger strike. This, obviously, is what the SP, Porompat, would like her to do, along with the entire establishment he represents. And this, equally obvious, is the last thing Irom Sharmila will do!

Having vented his ire, the SP reluctantly allows us permission for a visit, but directs us to the DG (Prisons) for further permission. We repair to the Central Jail office, where we are told to go to Sajiwa Central Jail, and take permission from there, too.

So we do the rounds of police stations and jails, a day after arriving in this breathtakingly beautiful state. The drive to Sajiwa Central Jail takes us out of Imphal town, through emerald-green paddy fields stretching towards hazy brown hills on all sides, a peaceful blue sky overhead. Within this pastel setting, emerge tall yellow jail buildings, jarringly out-of-place. We turn into a dirt road leading up to the jagged buildings. Security force personnel spring into sight. CRPF men are stationed here, and Manipur Rifles as well. Uniformed soldiers hang around chit-chatting, enjoying leisure time in the open grounds around the jail. Some eye us with interest, and faint insolence. The jail stands stiff and incongruous in the green-blue landscape, its barbed wiring designed to ensnarl errant prisoners. Sajiwa Central Jail is at the outskirts of Sajiwa village, amid fields cultivated by local people. I wonder how it would feel, what it would mean, to have a jail constructed in the garden of my home or in a neighbourhood park—and shudder at the images that loom up.

We are hungry, anxious and weary. We do not know whether we shall actually get to meet Sharmila, ever. Chewing *vaatin*, a crisp local savoury we pick up at a little shop, helps diffuse anxiety. Our jeep driver, a supportive presence who is in fact a computer programmer with a local NGO, kind enough to help us carry out our mission today, describes the ingredients and the virtues of vaatin. Local food is a passion with most Manipuris—for good reason.

The clouds begin to clear. The additional DG, Sajiwa Central Jail, sends an inspector with us, driving ahead on his motorcycle. We drive back to JN Hospital through the deceptively calm landscape. Familiar billboards on TB HIV/AIDS, vaccination and maternity care greet us again, as we approach the hospital. The inspector, self-important as is only to be expected, walks ahead of us, and we are led into the secret corridor, thence to Sharmila's room: Security Ward Number 2, JN Hospital.

༉

Sharmila's face crinkles up into a huge smile, then delighted laughter. She is pleased, and surprised. She had no inkling we are to visit, because nobody bothered to inform her. In the six weeks since she came from Delhi, nobody else has managed to pay her a visit. She gives me a warm hug, her body frail, all skin and bones. The portly inspector, momentarily hospitable, helps arrange red and blue plastic chairs near Sharmila's bed.

To my 'How are you?' she replies, 'I am fine,' and then slowly smiles and repeats, 'Fine!' I smile back at her, recalling my many visits in Delhi, when I asked the same question, and she made the same reply. A stereotypical polite exchange had grown poignant with meaning. She is on indefinite hunger strike, confined to a hospital bed, but rather than launch into a narrative about her ailments, she wants you to understand that she, *personally*, is fine.

She is keen to show me something. Almost breathless with excitement, she pulls out a notebook from beneath her pillow, 'I have written a poem in this. See.' She opens it to show page after page of poetry, in neat bold letters of a script I do not follow, a language I do not comprehend. 'I began the poem on Tuesday, March 20th,' she continues enthusiastically. 'I completed it on 17th of April—the day before yesterday. I was so happy yesterday. I finished my poem in twenty-eight days. It is a 1,010 line poem!'

'Is it about your life?' I ask, thumbing through the pages, wishing I could read the flowing Bengali script, in which Sharmila has written her Manipuri (Meiteilon) poem.

'No, it is about society. I wish I could read it to you. I wish you could read it. I would like you to read it.'

I request her to read out the first page. She reads willingly, her voice sonorous, chanting rather than merely reciting. She explains the meaning. The poem, 'Rebirth' or 'Reincarnation', begins, 'Today is Tuesday—the day on which I was born ...' and continues with a meditation on life, and the purpose of her existence here in this world, between birth and death. She wonders, 'For what has my Creator joined me with my family, my friends ... What have I to do?' She mentions feeling restless, then a little later, 'My mind is not concerned with my body organs ...' Her concern is with matters of greater import than this transient physical sheath.

She is alert as we discuss who could best translate her long poem into English. She has written a few hundred poems, most of which still await translation. Nearly a hundred, she says, are lying with CORE, an NGO in Imphal that has long been promising to publish them; others are with professors of literature, in Manipur and in Delhi. She does not have any copies of most of these poems. She requests me to hand over 'Rebirth' to a publisher she got to know in Delhi, and I promise to do so. 'You must keep a copy with you,' I urge her, and she agrees.

The conversation shifts to an operation she underwent a few days ago, to drain away excess fluid from her chin. Medical tape covers the spot. She says the stitches healed fast, but fluid has again accumulated. She will be taken to the nursing home for another check-up, and may be another surgery.

Light streams in from broad windows in the wall opposite Sharmila's bed. The windows provide a dismal view, the hospital courtyard resembling a junkyard, with piles of abandoned furniture lying any which way. Sharmila has pasted a number of cards and pictures on the walls beside, and behind, her. She exclaims agitatedly about losing a picture my daughter painted for her, which she had pasted next to her in the hospital in Delhi. Sharmila had relished the sketch of a reflective girl, a dog and a butterfly, watching a sunset. She says she brought it carefully from Delhi, saw it here among her books and papers, and then it disappeared.

Irom Singhjit had gone out leaving us with his sister. He bustles in, and Sharmila says she wants to talk to him about something very important. I ask if she'd like us to step out, but she says, 'No no no.' Singhjit stands at the foot of the bed and they exchange a few rapid sentences in Manipuri. Satisfied, he steps out, and she explains, 'There was a communication gap between us from the last few days in Delhi. I had not seen my brother after I was arrested. Today I have spoken to him, and that communication gap is finished.'

She points to a birthday card pasted next to her, sent by a friend, Charu Shankar. Sharmila turned thirty-five on 14 March. The card has a peacock, with a real peacock feather as the tail, and the message, '...You told me you wanted to hold a bird in your hands ... I made this bird for your birthday.'

Sharmila is excited again, and relates, 'It is unbelievable—but yesterday a bird flew in from the window and sat on my bed. I held it in my hands. I held it for some time, and then it flew away. It flew out of the window. I was so happy!'

She adds that it was a sparrow, and it flew in just after she had completed her poem. For a while we contemplate this magical event—was it real, or a dream?

Sharmila asks where we are living in Imphal, and whether we like the Manipuri curries. When I say we have not yet tasted any, she describes various curries, in lingering detail. Her favourite, *sagem pomba*, is made with fermented soya bean and various vegetables, roots and water plants. She recalls, 'I made it for Preeti and Justice Suresh and Colin in October 2000—when they came for the Human Rights Commission to Manipur. I made it at home, and brought it to the office.' She adds—a simple enough promise—'I will make sagem pomba for you one day,' and then a proud afterthought, 'I have some skill in cooking vegetables.'

I gaze at her in wonder: she who has not tasted food for the past six-and-a-half years, discussing food so easily, and so confidently talking about the day when she would cook again. I recall, with awe, several occasions in Delhi when I heard her ask a visitor, 'Have you had breakfast (or lunch)?' or when she would turn to me and say, 'There are bananas in the cupboard. Please take a banana.'

I ask whether she will write another poem, soon.

'No,' she replies.

'What will you do now that you have finished writing this poem?' I pursue the theme.

'Nothing,' she says. 'My mind is ... empty.'

After a pause she explains pensively, 'I am alone here. There is nobody most of the time. The nurses come in to feed me through the plastic tube. That is five times a day. At night one or two girls sleep on that bed'—indicating a bed, set against the wall. 'Nobody is here in the day. The nurses and the other girls, they do not talk to me. They are not supposed to talk to me.'

'Have you been doing your yoga?'

'Yes,' she grows happier, 'I do my yoga.' She practises yoga for several hours, spread through the day. Every morning she takes a walk up and down the corridor. 'I walk for two hours, barefoot. I do not wear any slippers or shoes; it is part of my pledge. Today I got up at 3 a.m. and went for my walk. It is very important. I keep healthy with my yoga and my walking. The head-stand keeps my senses alert, and my brain ... I do some 'hanging' postures, which help my digestion ... If I did not do these asanas I would not be well.'

We talk a little more, but all of a sudden the inspector, who has been sitting on the other bed, his back turned to us as he ate a sumptuous packed lunch, peremptorily calls for an end to this meeting. So far he has been nonchalant and easy-going. But now he rises briskly and barks out firmly, 'Bas. Ab band karo.' ('Enough. Now stop this.') Taken aback, I remind him we have permission for several hours' visit. He notes sagaciously, 'That is only on paper. A visit is only for one hour.' Since he is clearly in charge, and we have already been with Sharmila for over an hour, there is no scope for further argument. We linger for just a few minutes more.

We hand over a present from Delhi—a white sheet on which Lady Shri Ram College students have written out messages for Irom Sharmila, in bold blue, red and black. She eagerly scans the messages—young voices expressing solidarity:

- Justice needs to be ensured. There are no exceptions. Sonam
- Freedom and security for all. Vani
- Humanity is under siege. Raise your voice against AFSPA. Make India what it set out to be.
- Let's raise our voices against demonocracy. Gaurangi
- We believe in what's right and U R right.
- Stand for justice with the people of Manipur and Sharmila. Radha
- Act on the Act—Fast. Shivani
- AFSPA is state-sponsored terrorism.
- We are with you Sharmila. Shayoni
- It's time we think about it seriously.
- For humanity and for hope. Akanksha
- Down with state violence! Repeal AFSPA. Stop the state from being so violent toward the people. Sunaina
- This is BARBARISM. Kinni
- Let's join our hands and rise. Prittha.

Leaving her with dozens of such messages, we walk away. It is with a heavy heart that I leave this plucky woman, knowing not how she will be within those 'jail hospital' walls, nor when I shall see her next. The prison grill clicks shut behind us, and I imagine the guards heave a sigh of relief as they continue with their routine, undisturbed. It may be weeks, even months, before Sharmila is allowed another visitor.

The law allows anybody in custody, be it an undertrial or a convict, regular visits by family members, friends and lawyers. Sharmila is not permitted this basic freedom, although there is no court order commanding her isolation. Were she actually a candidate for suicide, such detention would surely have further pushed her into suicidal depression. But she carries on miraculously, guided by an extraordinary inner strength, cheerful and focussed, in spite of lonely confinement, day in and day out, year after year.

❦

Two years later, in November 2009, I am in Imphal for the Festival of Hope, Peace and Justice, organized by local people and organizations. The first edition of *Burning Bright* is released; as a consequence, the authorities deny me permission to visit Irom Sharmila. Writing a book on her and on Manipur makes me persona non grata in the eyes of the state government. More importantly, their effort to isolate Irom Sharmila, and break her spirit through isolating her, is palpable. After this experience, I continuously urge a number of lawyers and activists, to take up this one issue on an urgent and priority basis. Activists of Save Sharmila Solidarity Campaign brought the issue to the notice of NHRC—which finally (after its own special rapporteur, a retired DIG of police, was denied permission to meet Sharmila) intervened. Due to this intervention, in late 2013, though she is still locked up in her cell, at least she is able to meet visitors more frequently.

A PURE ACTIVIST FOR HUMAN RIGHTS

Victorious Worm

Since death hasn't visited me, I'm able to see
Kanglei,[58] the mirror of my vision
On the new page of history
Written in red ink.

In the battle fought between God and worm
Saying worm has killed God
The enticing nature of man
Is worshipped as godly by one and all

A dirty worm like me
Hates, like enemies, those
Who gain by sinning against the Almighty
Darkness prevails everywhere in the end.

—Irom Sharmila[59]

As Irom Sharmila persists in struggle, the government adamantly refuses to attend to the issues she is raising. Rather, its attempt is to ignore and physically isolate her, interpret her protest as a criminal offence, and lock her away as if she were a hardened criminal.

Nationally and internationally, she has been hailed as a defender of human rights. The convenor of Manipur People's Union for Civil Liberties (PUCL) pays rich tribute to her, noting, 'She is the only one at the moment who I think is a pure activist of "human rights".'[60]

Sharmila's incarceration provides living proof of the pervasive denial of human rights in Manipur today. A slew of organizations across the country have spoken out in defence of Sharmila and her protest, and against AFSPA. On 5 October 2006, Y.P. Chibbar, General Secretary of PUCL, said, '... She represents the pain the people of Manipur have suffered, especially because of the Armed Forces Special Powers Act. The PUCL appeals to all defenders of Human Rights to rally round her to lend her support in this centenary year of Mahatma Gandhi's satyagraha.'[61]

Lawyers from the HRLN have been arguing Sharmila's case in court. The Asian Human Rights Commission has painstakingly documented human rights violations in the state. The Indian Social Action Forum (INSAF) held a national convention in September 2007 on 'State Repression in India and People's Resistance (State Against its own Citizens)', in which activists, journalists and lawyers highlighted people's resistance in different parts of the country. Sociologists and political scientists are enquiring into human rights violations in Manipur and other parts of the North-East, Chhattisgarh, Jammu and Kashmir, and West Bengal, and pointing out elements of state fascism in the body politic. The state has arrested and imprisoned several leading civil rights activists, notably Binayak Sen, an active PUCL member who for decades ran a hospital serving the poor among indigenous people in Chhattisgarh.[62]

Human rights activists based in Manipur, in organizations such as HRA and the Meira Paibis, are among Irom Sharmila's closest associates. Her brother Irom Singhjit, busy mobilizing support for the cause while she is imprisoned, avers, 'I am not an activist. I am a warrior!' He dissociates himself from stereotypical modern activism that is often devoid of thoughtful reflection; and lays claim to an older, locally rooted way of defending the motherland.

In October 2007, United NGOs Mission, Manipur, sent a plea to the United Nations Committee on the Elimination of Racial Discrimination (CERD), Geneva, alleging that AFSPA was responsible for 'gross violations of indigenous peoples' basic human rights ... while the perpetrators enjoy *de jure* impunity'. The plea also noted that armed opposition groups contribute to the cycle of violence and human rights abuse in the region. In March 2007, CERD deliberated on the United NGOs Mission's plea, and advocated that the 'draconian' legislation of 1958 be replaced with 'a more humane act'. The United Nations Human Rights Committee (UNHRC) has noted that AFSPA is incompatible with the International Covenant on Civil and Political Rights (ICCPR), ratified by India in 1979. Many members of the Committee have expressed shock at the existence of such legislation in India. Nobel Laureate Shirin Ebadi continues to frequently represent Sharmila's cause at international human rights fora.

ॐ

In May 2007, the citizens of Gwangju, South Korea, awarded Irom Sharmila the Gwangju Human Rights Award, instituted in memory of those martyred in the town while fighting against tyranny. Celebrating the spirit of the 18 May 1980 uprising against dictatorship, the Award recognizes individuals, groups and institutions that contribute significantly to promoting and advancing human rights, democracy and peace. It is, today, the most prestigious human rights award in South Asia.

Although it was a signal honour conferred upon an Indian citizen, the Indian government did not give Irom Sharmila permission to travel to Gwangju, to receive the award. Her brother Irom Singhjit went instead, and spoke on her behalf, on 18 May 2007:

Daughter and Sister of All the People of Manipur

I am here today on behalf of a woman who was once just my sister and for whom the pursuit of justice, equality and basic human rights have become a mission for the last six years. She cannot be present here today amongst the distinguished gathering as she remains in judicial custody.

A small but resolute voice of Manipur finding a resonance in the distant Far East and the struggle of Gwangju is indeed a testimony to the umbilical bond of the Asian peoples far and wide.

Sharmila, adoringly called Memtombi, is the youngest sibling among the nine of us. I choose to address her as only Sharmila, as she has chosen her people and suffering population across humanity as her family.

Here I stand to accept this prestigious award, as Sharmila wanted, on behalf of the indomitable Meira Paibis and the people of Manipur whose relentless struggle for the repeal of the Armed Forces Special

Powers Act still continues. Theirs is a movement for uprooting the Act from the face of the earth and not just the removal of the Act from Manipur for, as they say, they do not want other peoples to suffer as they have suffered.

I shall take the liberty to also mention the sufferings of other peoples in the subcontinent such as the Nagas, the Assamese and the Tripuris, all disqualified by the Indian state from being mainstream Indians through the Act.

As we gather here in Gwangju in memory of the countless sufferings and the defiant human spirit, Sharmila lies alone strapped in involuntary feeding in a closely guarded room of a hospital religiously hoping for an end, not of her self-imposed fast, but of the discriminatory Act.

As a child, she was somewhat withdrawn or somehow different from the rest. But I never thought those subtle differences would later develop into what she is today. Born in the turbulent '70s, Sharmila grew up in a Manipur whose people were undergoing a process of rediscovering its identity, historical pride and lost nationhood.

I shall not dwell much on the wounds of the past or how a proud and independent nation was reduced to a centrally administered region in 1949. But I must say wounds that refuse to heal with time or democratic pretensions of the state brought insurgency in 1964, and so also a series of student or civil society movements since the early '70s.

India, instead of democratic redressal of the issues raised by the various movements, brought in the Armed Forces

Special Powers Act to the whole of Manipur in 1980.
I must not forget to mention here, at a time when the
Korean people were pushing for a break from the past
chained in military rule, Manipur was sliding towards an
oppressive regime.

Civil society resistance began with a petition challenging
the constitutionality of the Act in 1980 itself to the
highest court of India. But, it remained unheard and
unresolved for seventeen long years till 1997, when the
Court rejected the petition.

I am not an activist and I am not here to relate the
untold sufferings under the Act. But, I must ask, why
should there be a separate law governing the peoples of
the North-east?

Today, I cannot but mention the indomitable spirit
of the Meira Paibis of Manipur who have been in the
forefront of the movement for repeal of the Act and
protection of human rights in the region.

Sharmila, a young poet and a girl who had just left
high school, was deeply pained by the culture of violence
perpetrated by security forces upon innocent civilians, a
culture nurtured by the Indian state with impunity.

Come 2nd November 2000, ten innocent civilians
were mowed down by irate personnel of the security
forces in a bus stand near Malom, a suburban area
adjoining Imphal city, in retaliation to an insurgent
attack.

The incident became a defining moment for Sharmila.
She set up camp at the massacre site and began her fast.
Sharmila remains ever steadfast in her resolve and unique
protest with a yearning for more democratic space and
equality in Manipur and the North-east.

I must also mention here, the historic protest of twelve Manipuri women disrobing at the gate of a city military station and the supreme sacrifice of a student leader torching himself in 2004 amidst widespread public upheaval seeking repeal of the Act.

When the news of Gwangju award was delivered to her, she said—'Go and accept the award on behalf of the people of Manipur. The movement needs it. We must thank Gwangju and the world for the solidarity and support.'

So here I am. For I sincerely believe this solidarity and recognition would bring a new vigour to the movement for justice, equality and basic human rights.

I am also here to insist upon a search for a new beginning where we can all live together with dignity and as qualified citizens.[63]

Lawyer Preeti Verma spoke at the function, noting that Irom Sharmila Chanu is an extraordinary example of civil courage. By having consistently 'refused to give up on her belief that not guns but peaceful protest will make the nation engage with the North-East's plight', she has become an important symbol in the struggle against oppression. Verma hoped the Gwangju award would pave the way to create more opportunities to fight against inequalities in the North-East and elsewhere. Anni Raja, general secretary, National Federation of Indian Women, present at the occasion, said that Sharmila's heroic struggle is a mark in the women's movement, worldwide.

Professor Rhee Hong Gil, chairperson of the 18 May Memorial Foundation, Gwangju, noted, 'History is not complete. Democracy is not complete. Democracy has to be preserved and made better and better. There is always the fear that it will be crushed or co-opted or manipulated. We have to be alert. The anniversary of the uprising and the prize commemoration is a reminder that the struggle for democracy and human rights must continue.' The award honoured 'the unflagging efforts of Irom Sharmila and others who are striving to attain democracy, human rights and ethnic conciliation by peaceful means'. Everyone, said Professor Gil, is watching India's future: Will it succumb to corporate dictatorship, sacrificing human rights and social justice at the altar of false gods?

Irom Sharmila joined a galaxy of great legends of pro-democracy and human rights struggles in Asia, who received the Gwangju Human Rights Award in previous years—Nobel Laureate Aung San Suu Kyi of Myanmar; Xanana Gusmao, President of East Timor; the Korean Association of Bereaved Families for Democracy; Wardah Hafidz of the Urban Poor Consortium in Indonesia; Dandeniya Gamage Jayanthi of the Monument for the Disappeared, Sri Lanka; Malalai Joya of Afghanistan; and Basil Fernando of the Asian Human Rights Commission, Hong Kong.

☸

Contemporary writing in Manipur is replete with images of people suffering human rights violations. Leibakalai, a poor hard-working woman, returns home one evening to find both daughter and son killed by security forces in a combing operation. She becomes mentally deranged and takes to wandering the streets, picking a fight with any security man she sees. In another village, Lairek, an elderly woman is arrested and imprisoned, simply because she took in a young boy who knocked at her door one night, wiped his gaping wounds, and fed him scraps of food.[64]

To curb rampant violation of human rights, international bodies have laid down substantive human rights standards, especially from the 1940s onwards. Attempts to regulate interstate relations made rapid headway, while laws regulating intra-state conflict lagged behind. States repeatedly raised the bogie of 'interference with internal affairs' to keep regulation at bay. Intra-state violations of human rights therefore remained virtually screened from the purview of international norms. But with determined efforts, global consensus gradually emerged prohibiting nation states from killing their own citizens.

The special powers AFSPA grants security personnel, to kill civilians indiscriminately, are globally unacceptable. International complaint procedures started operating in the 1970s. These procedures include provision for an individual to condemn human rights violations by one's own state, and pursue investigation by international tribunals. The 'right to intervene' in the case of universally accepted violations, such as summary executions, is recognized as a humanitarian right.[65]

Militarism and war result in pervasive denial of human rights. The UN tirelessly reiterates that humanity must realize the adverse impact of the arms race and pervasive use of military options. Current debates reveal that over 25 per cent of developing countries' debt burden originates in military expenditure. The development toll of military expenditure is a legitimate human rights issue: there are strong arguments in favour of converting a large part of military funds to meet basic civilian needs. India allocates nearly 15 per cent of budgetary expenditure on 'defence', with much lower amounts spent on welfare, education or health. As human rights organizations point out, some of the defence expenditure works *against* the interests of ordinary citizens, by inflicting human rights casualties within the civilian population, as in Manipur today. Yet the build-up of arms and armaments, including nuclear arsenal, is carrying on at a rapid pace.

In a democratic world, citizens ought to decide whether or not they want the earth's resources to be used up in accumulation of destructive weaponry. The world Irom Sharmila dreams of is a world where power is distributed evenly, ordinary people wield control over their own lives, and actively participate in all the most significant global decisions.

SOLIDARITY: THE POWER OF THE POWERLESS

Anti-AFSPA Day is observed in Imphal on 11 September every year, since it is the day AFSPA was promulgated in 1958. In 2006 the day was marked by a few hundred people participating in a seminar on 'Democracy as A Lived Experience'. They signed a petition expressing solidarity with Irom Sharmila in her courageous protest, and demanded withdrawal of AFSPA.

On 11 September 2007, a global fast was held by human rights activists, students and common citizens, in solidarity with Irom Sharmila and her cause. Sympathizers staged demonstrations simultaneously in six nations of the world—India, Pakistan, Bangladesh, the USA, the UK and Saudi Arabia. The solidarity fast and simultaneous demonstrations were coordinated by the National Alliance of People's Movements (NAPM), a joint body of about 200 organizations working on civil and democratic rights in different parts of India, representing a very wide range of struggles against oppression.

More than 500 people from various walks of life took part in the demonstration at Imphal, and over fifty sat on a five-day hunger strike, expressing support for Irom Sharmila's steadfast protest. Manipur Forward Youth Front (MFYF) president, Sapamcha Kangleipal, said, 'The issue of AFSPA and human rights violations in Manipur has become globalized and we will continue to support the protest.'

NAPM members met Irom Sharmila in the Security Ward of JN Hospital. Noting that all peace-loving people of the world ought to support the struggle against AFSPA, activists pledged unstinting support to her campaign. They remarked that her struggle is 'far above any human capacity and endurance'. Sharmila told them that no amount of pressure or requests will change her mind: 'I will not retrace my steps nor suspend my agitation, until my aspiration is achieved or realized.' She expressed gratitude for their concern and support.[66] She also requested them to convey a letter to Congress (I) leader Sonia Gandhi. NAPM activists subsequently handed over the letter to Sonia Gandhi's office in New Delhi. However, Sharmila never received any reply.

☙

Irom Sharmila founded 'Just Peace' in September 2007, an organization devoted to carrying forward processes for restoration of peace and justice in this embattled state, and elsewhere. She gave the cash component of the Gwangju Human Rights Award, a sum of about Rs 1,200,000 ($25,000), to the organization. Just Peace will continue her work for ending human rights violations, engaging in advocacy at different levels, lobbying for critical shifts in national policies, and transformation in human thinking and consciousness. Just Peace held its first outreach event in Imphal on 6 November 2007: a workshop on International Humanitarian Law, disseminating crucial information to journalists, lawyers and activists. The event also commemorated completion of seven years of Irom Sharmila's fast.

On 7 March 2008, Irom Sharmila was released, after completing one year in judicial custody, the maximum punishment for attempted suicide. She continued her fast outside, surrounded by supporters. They asked her to address a public gathering the next day—International Women's Day. She has earlier been recognized as one of the most eminent 'Peacewomen' of the world—included in a group of 1,000 leading women worldwide, who are working towards peace.

On the morning of 8 March, a large crowd of women, men and children gathered to hear her. She was just about to begin speaking, when the police came to arrest her. The people requested the police to allow her to speak, but to no avail. Although 8 March is a day to celebrate women's struggles all over the world, in Manipur, Irom Sharmila was not allowed to address her people. But as thousands surged to the grounds, she could feel their palpable support.

On 21 September, International Peace Day, the organization Kriti held a panel discussion in New Delhi, on the theme 'Manufacturing Peace'. There was a lively discussion on diverse movements for peace and justice, and the situation in Manipur, with a focus on Irom Sharmila and people's struggles against AFSPA.

On 10 December 2008, International Human Rights Day, women's organizations in Manipur, coordinated by the Meira Paibis, came together as 'Sharmila Kanba Lup' (Save Sharmila Group) to launch an indefinite hunger strike—and continued over the next year. Thousands of women took part over the next few years. Their central slogan is 'Save Sharmila, Repeal AFSPA'. A number of women from nearby areas arrive every morning and sit-in for the entire day undertaking a solidarity fast. Another set of women from another locality replaces them next day. The movement is self-propelling, with many women coming in just by reading about the protest in local newspapers. This remarkable relay fast takes place in a makeshift bamboo shelter at PDA complex, next to JN Hospital in Imphal.

NAPM extended support to the anti-AFSPA struggle, with activists from other parts of India, such as Sandeep Pandey and Bela Bhatia, coming to Imphal in a strong expression of continuing solidarity. NAPM has also spread the news to a wider circle of supporters.

On 19 January 2009, Irom Sharmila submitted a written application to government authorities seeking permission to meet media persons to discuss AFSPA in Manipur. However, her application was rejected by the state government's home department. In mid-February 2009, a literary group from Thoubal district launched a poster campaign to show solidarity with Irom Sharmila, adding strength to her demand for the repeal of AFSPA. On 27 February, a broad alliance of various social organizations sent a memorandum to the President of India, Ms Pratibha Patil, seeking the withdrawal of AFSPA, and drawing attention to 'the deteriorating condition of satyagrahi Irom Sharmila'. The alliance included Manipur Students Association Delhi, Manipur Women Gun Survivors' Network, All India Women's Studies Association, South Asian Forum for Human Rights, Asha Parivaar, Reach Out, NAPM, Indian Social Action Forum, Indian Social Security, Human Rights Alert, The Other Media, Human Rights Law Network, Saheli Women's Group, Jagriti Mahila Samiti, Centre for Women's Development Studies, and students from Delhi University and Jamia Millia Islamia. The alliance organized a candlelight vigil in New Delhi on 7 March and a meeting on the occasion of International Women's Day, to highlight the urgency of saving Irom Sharmila, repealing AFSPA and similar draconian laws in the North-East and Jammu and Kashmir, as well as bringing justice to all victims of violence, whether perpetrated by the state or by insurgent organizations.

On 7 March 2009, Irom Sharmila was again released. As Meira Paibis and others received her, an emotional Sharmila said, 'I come back to the arms of my mothers, the mothers of Manipur.' She joined protestors at the PDA complex in Porompat. She continued her fast, and when police and commandos came to re-arrest her on the morning of 9 March, she put up no resistance. When Meira Paibis asked her to say a few words, she intoned softly, 'I wanted to continue my struggle outside the jail. Now, they have come to arrest me. I don't have anything left to say.'

Meira Paibis, who stayed the night with Sharmila, said the human rights crusader spoke about corruption in the administration, and need for women to take part in decision making. 'She did not sleep for long during the two nights. She spent the time talking to us. Her courage and stamina are beyond our imagination,' said P. Sumita Devi, a Meira Paibi leader.

On 10 March 2009, a delegation submitted a memorandum to the governor demanding that Sharmila's life be saved, AFSPA repealed, and peace and harmony restored in the state. Ima Janaki, convenor of the Sharmila Kanba Lup, announced that along with continuation of the relay hunger strike, their stir would be intensified with street corner meetings, posters and pamphlets. The demand for removal of AFSPA from Manipur would henceforth be extended to demanding removal of AFSPA from the entire North-East. Co-convenor Ima Momon informed that relay hunger strike would also be staged at Wabagai Lamkhai during the upcoming Yaoshang festival, and appealed to all to observe two-minute silence during the sports meet at Yaoshang, as a mark of solidarity and respect.

༈

People continue to rally around Irom Sharmila, year after year, moved by her unwavering commitment. A variety of persons, groups and movements, across party, sectarian and ethnic lines, has forged links with her. Her allegiance is to universal principles; she represents no particular organization, community or party.

Most people are deeply impressed by her endurance and commitment. Through it all, she has retained a sense of perspective, and deep humility. She believes that every person has the potential to act as a rational being, and make a difference to the larger scheme of things. Claiming to be no more important than a lowly worm, she acknowledges the significance of her struggle, for she is acting as a rational being, in accordance with her conscience. Each person's contribution is important, she emphasizes, in the search to create a better world.

At a time of ever-sharpening identity politics, her example illustrates the possibility of reaching across boundaries, to touch the overlaps in human experience. Cultural, ethnic or national identities need not preclude wider sympathy and empathy, or betray the fact that we all belong to a common humanity.

༈

Irom Sharmila is strong. Were she weak, the state would have completely ignored her struggle, and let her starve to death. By responding to her protest with anger and fear, the state is in effect acknowledging her strength. In February 2006, when the home ministry, Government of India, strategically prevented her return to Manipur, keeping her stashed away in a Delhi hospital, while assembly elections were held in her state, she cried, in a moment of frustration, 'I am powerless! They are not letting me go to Manipur when I want to go!'

'They' used brute power to keep her away from the arena. But in a strange sense, this actually confirms her power: if she were not influential, they would not be afraid of her. The government's mighty sword can control her physical mobility. But her power soars and spreads, despite her capture and physical entrapment. Her power spreads through people's hearts and minds, awakening a spark: call it social conscience, or political will. She represents 'the power of the powerless'— an evocative term, which Victor Havel used while discussing Myanmarese leader Aung San Suu Kyi.

The power of the powerless refers to the invincible force of millions of people, who seek to live in peace. They work hard, and want a share in the fruits of their labour. Irom Sharmila speaks for all these people.

Her activism is no flash in the pan. Rather, it is embedded in people's resistance, over the centuries, to unjust power. Her roots go deep—roots she will not abandon, even as she grows wings.

She demonstrates the power of one: linked, inextricably, to a collective aspiration. One individual can stand up against the power of an empire.

Her moral and spiritual force is working its magic quietly. Her undying commitment and unique act of continuous self-denial have lit a flame that burns bright in a million hearts. Most of us would like her to give up the fast, because we feel the sacrifice is too great. However, she shrugs aside any such suggestion, always expressing determination to continue until the demand is met.

☙

The media is particularly crucial in a 'quiet' protest like Irom Sharmila's, which relies on non-violent and democratic methods. Communicating information to a wider domain of like-minded people is of critical significance since it can help consolidate and broad-base the struggle. The government, at present reluctant to repeal AFSPA, may have to bow down to mounting public pressure. After all, an elected government cannot remain totally immune to public opinion.

It is sometimes assumed that those struggling for people's issues should have no interest in media attention, but this is a very short-sighted view. In fact, people's issues ought to be accorded priority space, their struggles especially covered. In an era of globalized market-driven media, winning space for people-oriented issues constitutes a major battle in itself.

By providing information and inspiring discussion in the public sphere, the media can build opinion in favour of a cause. It can educate, motivate and keep the issue alive in people's minds, generating a non-violent force that supports, and even lobbies for, a cause. Public pressure exerted by this constituency is what finally induces the oppressors to pay heed.

The media, as watchdog of democracy, ought to play the role of highlighting important people's issues and struggles, but most media today is commercialized and sensation-oriented. Regional biases exacerbate the situation, for instance, B.B.

Sharma, head of the North-East Region News Unit, All India Radio, remarks that there is a 'prolonged communication gap' between the north-eastern states and the mainland.[67] At the same time, a number of specialized journals, news networks and committed journalists focus on bringing out in-depth stories on people's movements and issues such as food security, human rights and land alienation. Mainstream newspapers pick up some of these issues, providing outreach to a wider readership.

Gandhi used existing media, and launched a number of publications, to build public opinion on burning issues. His newspapers were deliberate vehicles to communicate news of non-violent campaigns, from the early years in South Africa up to the momentous freedom struggle in India. He realized the essential and integral role of the media in the success of political and social campaigns. During the Salt Satyagraha, for instance, 700 volunteers were beaten up by the police, 320 hospitalized with injuries, while two died. Journalists present were moved by the courage of the volunteers who kept coming forward in spite of facing ruthless blows. The media across the world carried the story. The brutal assault continued for several days, with no visible softening of the opponents' hearts. Yet the state did change the legislation regarding salt, through a circuitous and indirect route. Sensitive media reportage helped build public opinion, and the authorities found they were fast losing legitimacy in the eyes of people, in India and elsewhere. Because of this they gave in, making the required policy and legislative changes.[68]

When Irom Sharmila came from Imphal to New Delhi in October 2006, her motive was to reach out to more people, directly and through media. Local media had reported her campaign over the years, but national and international media seldom picked up the news. Local dailies like the *Sangai Express* and *Imphal Free Press* routinely covered events in her campaign, and regional newspapers such as the *North-East Sun* frequently reported milestones. But the campaign deserved wider publicity, in India and elsewhere.

Once she was in New Delhi, journalists and camera crew from numerous media houses could easily approach her. The very 'escape' from Imphal became a peg, a newsworthy event with a hint of a cloak-and-dagger action and suspense. A lot of people learnt about her struggle for the first time, through write-ups and images on mainstream media. Others, clued in and already aware of her struggle, were able to read detailed stories in *Tehelka*, *Communalism Combat*, *Civil Society*, *Hindu*, *Telegraph* and a range of other publications. Reuters, BBC, UNI and PTI carried brief stories at one point or the other, during her Delhi sojourn. Nobel Laureate Shirin Ebadi's visit drew further attention to Irom Sharmila's cause, as did the discussion around her condition in Indian Parliament.

Select audiences had already viewed *Tales from the Margins*, made by independent film-maker Kavita Joshi in 2005, and screened at several documentary film festivals. Other than describing her campaign, it has powerful images of the Meira Paibi nude protest against Thangjam Manorama's rape and murder, as well as of Irom Sharmila in JN hospital, Imphal. NDTV and other television channels interviewed Sharmila when she was in Delhi, and aired brief news stories, while CNN IBN prepared a well-researched half-hour documentary on Sharmila's struggle, in late 2006. All this helped keep the issues alive in the consciousness of a wide audience.

But after a couple of months of Sharmila's stay in Delhi, media interest flagged. By the time she left Delhi to return to Imphal in early March 2007, the media hardly paid her any attention.

Immediately after her return to Imphal, local newspapers reported her arrest at Nupilan Memorial Building, photographed against the familiar frieze of fierce protesters of 1939. This memorial statue, symbol of women's resistance to exploitative power, became a dramatic backdrop to her arrest. After this report, however, the local and regional press covered her struggle only when there was a particular event, such as her trial on 11 May 2007 at New Delhi's Patiala House Court, the Gwangju Award of May 2007, the solidarity fast by NAPM and MFYF in September 2007, her release and re-arrest in March 2008, and again in March 2009, and the relay hunger strike by Sharmila Kanba Lup activists, beginning December 2008.

Swiss journal *Le Courier* carried an article by Marc-Oliviera Parlatano in April 2007, noting that Irom Sharmila's is the longest political fast ever recorded—totting up to 2,552 days by 13 April 2007! Describing 'the struggle of a young woman who keeps fasting for peace', he called her 'a living icon of liberty-famished Indians'. He mused, 'It is utopic, in the present military and political environment, but at least, in war-torn Manipur, a handful of citizens do not capitulate in front of guns ...' He rued the fact that she was still almost unknown in Europe.

One medium that consistently carries stories on Sharmila and anti-AFSPA struggles is the Internet. Dedicated websites like e-pao.net and manipuronline store a wealth of information. A few blogs add a personal dimension to the collective public response. On 11 October 2006, one Sudeep posted a short piece, 'Is Sharmila Irom Real?', in his blog. He evocatively describes sharing information about Irom Sharmila's fast with his friends, and their response. Friends were '... concerned about me, not the lady. That I better stay away from such delicate issues ...' Then he pens his own response: 'Life is precious. Yes, my life is precious. What about many other lives that hang on this particular Act?' His blog reveals how a sensitive citizen may be strongly drawn to such a cause, and yet experience fears and apprehensions that discourage direct involvement.[69]

Recognizing the power of the media, underground groups in Manipur try to muzzle the press, sometimes literally at gunpoint. Local newspapers face the difficult, often impossible, task of appeasing various underground groups. Almost every day there are threats over the phone or Internet, from proscribed outfits. The Manipur Hill Journalists Union has received many such threats. In early October 2007, PREPAK (People's Revolutionary Party of Kangleipak) threatened editors of major dailies with dire consequences if they failed to publish news of its raising day ceremony. A rival underground group communicated to newspapers that if they published news of the ceremony, all editors, reporters and staff would be shot dead. Newspapers in Imphal launched a strike after both underground groups exerted continuous pressure on the editors. The All Manipur Working Journalists' Union, and the Editors'

Forum Manipur, decided to cease newspaper publication because of the terror they faced. Publication resumed only when the two underground groups gave written undertakings that they would not harass the press.[70] Editors resolved not to submit to any diktat from any quarter to publish or not publish any news. The state government had from time to time curbed freedom of the press, with frequent harassment of working journalists. On 17 November 2008, Konsam Rishikanta of the *Imphal Free Press* was shot dead by unknown gunmen—the sixth journalist to be killed in Manipur since 1993. When the media aired its suspicion about involvement of state police in the killing, there was no response from the state; journalists sat on a protest strike for thirteen days, taking out a silent rally, in which hundreds of citizens participated, on 26 November. According to Anjulika T. Samon in *Infochange Agenda*, the state Cabinet conceded the demand for a CBI enquiry into the killing, only after the intervention of the Editor's Guild of India, on 1 December.[71]

On 15 August 2004, a young man, Pebam Chittaranjan, had committed self-immolation in front of Kangla Gate, protesting AFSPA and state violence. Somebody captured his last moments on camera, and the local channel, ISTV, aired the footage. The state responded by taking ISTV off the air.

Underground groups have banned all national and international channels from operating in Manipur, as well as Bollywood and foreign films, alleging that these have a corrupting influence on Manipuri society. Nobody dares to go against their diktat.

Mainstream national newspapers and channels face no grave risk from underground groups, yet they carry precious little information on issues concerning the North-East. While violent incidents such as bombing are sometimes reported, underlying factors and ongoing processes, particularly popular democratic struggles, are for the large part ignored.

☖

Dramatist Ratan Thiyyam's production *Nine Hills One Valley* depicts militarization and army violence in Manipur, and fervently argues for peace. The play begins with seven wise men, *Maichousing*, carriers of history and culture, being shaken by nightmares. Sons run from a barrage of bullets, desperately seeking the safety of mothers' arms. Time, a howling demon, disfigures sacred dancers of the Raas Lila. Newspapers reduce atrocities to ephemeral headlines. The Maichousing begin writing new *puyas* or books of wisdom, outlining principles of justice, governance, loyalty and obligation, and calling for liberation of the mind from tyranny and oppression. They urge us to look deeply within our souls to find the key to end the restlessness that has enveloped human societies. At the end of *Nine Hills One Valley*, lamps are lit on the hilltops and in the valley—tiny lights of hope, the stage ablaze, reminding people that peace is still possible.

Reflecting on another of his plays, *Uttar Priyadarshi*, about King Ashoka's conversion to non-violence, Thiyyam explains, 'For years I have been concentrating on war based plays because, given the situation in Manipur, we must present arguments for peace and solidarity … As an individual, I feel I must get control. Through theatre, I try to share it with my audience, as if to say, "Let us think together." … I always felt one should try to stop this kind of violence, which is affecting the next generation.'

For Thiyyam, his perspective is not a matter of choice; it is an imperative of contemporary life:

This is the condition of modern man: that you live somewhere, but you are compelled to think about the world—because you cannot be separated, or stand aloof from the problems of the world. The sufferings I am facing in this small place are not different from what is happening elsewhere. Suppose oil is burning in Kuwait or in Iraq; that does not mean that I will not suffer because I am in another corner of the globe. Sitting in Manipur, I think about the Gaza Strip, I think about Israel or Palestine, or America, about Afghanistan, about Pakistan and its relationship with India, Kashmir, bomb blasts in Bali. Globalization impinges on your own identity as a modern man and also on your native identity.[72]

Independent theatre, documentary films, the Internet and specialized publications help bring significant news and analyses into the public sphere, thus contributing to an alternative politics. Fearless media provides an essential channel for information. A play like *Meira Paibi* written by dramatist Civic Chandran in Kerala, was performed dozens of times, as part of a rally for peace from Kerala to Imphal, in 2010. Subsequently, it has been adapted as *Le Mashaale* (Taking the Burning Torces), and performed as a one-person act, extremely powerfully, by a young actor called S.V. Ojas.

The daily news we get is largely 'manufactured', yet responsible and committed media does exist, communicating serious issues, helping plant seeds of hope amidst pervasive despair and cynicism.

Foreign journalists are banned, by the special laws prevailing in Manipur, from visiting large parts of the state. They require a Restricted Area Permit to enter and travel in these areas. Human rights activists aver that this requirement prevents foreign media from investigating human rights abuse first-hand, thus drawing a thick curtain preventing the world from observing and learning about the ground situation in Manipur.

The mainstream national media zeroed in on the nude protests of July 2004, attracted no doubt by the sensation effect of women's public disrobing. International media too picked up the story and flashed it across the world. Thus due to this event, at least some news of the rampant injustice and violence trickled out to the rest of the world. Similarly, Irom Sharmila's 'escape' to Delhi roused media interest, which helped generate human interest and understanding for her cause.

Sympathizers have adopted various modes of communication to take forward the cause. They circulate pamphlets, such as the 'REPEAL OF AFSPA' UPDATE, in August 2007, encouraging democratic-minded citizens to raise their voices against 'injustices under AFSPA and the continued harassment of Irom Sharmila'. It urges respect for Irom Sharmila's peaceful struggle, withdrawal of restrictions on her mobility and freedom, implementation of recommendations of the Justice Jeevan Reddy Committee and Administrative Reforms Commission, and accountability from the armed forces. Brought out by Reachout, Human Rights Law Network, and Saheli, the pamphlet informs that those keen to support can sign an online petition, or send letters to the Indian prime minister, President, home minister, defence minister, labour minister, chairperson of the Human Rights Commission, Manipur chief minister and governor of Manipur. It adds, 'You can write directly to Sharmila and send her messages of solidarity at—Irom Sharmila Chanu, Security Ward, Jawaharlal Nehru Hospital, Porompat, Imphal: 795001, Manipur.'

When the TV channel CNN IBN invited viewers' votes for the 'Indian of the Year' award, 2006–7, a blog carried a write-up on 2 May 2007, 'My Indian of the Six Years'. The blogger, Anasuya, cast her vote for Irom Sharmila, 'the poet, the activist ... the woman who has been on a protest fast against the *Armed Forces Special Powers Act* for the past six years ...'[73]

Monisha Behal, senior activist, North East Network (NEN), is quoted in the same blog, appreciating an article about Irom Sharmila in *Femina* (14 February 2007), a women's magazine. Says Behal, 'I read the piece and saw a small message at the end of the final page: DO YOU SUPPORT IROM'S WAY OF FIGHTING THE AUTHORITIES? SMS us your replies at 3636 ... I hope very much that this new technique of the media will do some magic to a woman who wants to live, see and enjoy the beauty of the world.'

☙

Over the years media has kept in touch with the issue, often playing a critical role, for instance when she is released or re-arrested, or comes to Delhi for a court hearing. Protests receive some media coverage as well. Her re-arrest by police in Imphal in August 2014 was, for the first time, telecast over television nationally, sent shock waves across the country—it is one thing to hear about a person's arrest, and another to see a frail and gentle woman being brutally arrested by a posse of police personnel. International media too has maintained interest in the situation, and newspapers/journals carry the story from time to time—in Japan and Spain, Hong Kong and Sweden . . . BBC takes it up, so does Al Jazeera . . . though sporadically, yet the story has slowly made a place for itself.

Apart from www.epao.net and www.manipuronline, Internet resources on the theme include websites such as www.sangaiexpress.com; www.northeasttoday.in; www.hrw. org; www.kanglaonline.com; www.kracktivist.org; and blogs include repealafspa.blogspot.in; justpeacefoundation.blogspot. in and kavitajoshi.blogspot.in.

Thus media has responded, in its own way, to Irom Sharmila's struggle. Strategic communication by supporters, committed activists and media professionals, has contributed to the campaign by bringing out significant information, publicizing important events, and articulating issues of common concern. This has helped draw more people into the circle of sympathizers, creating a wider constituency that is aware of the issues, and cares about what happens.

It is by such means that the powerless begin to shed their helplessness, and, through informed opinion and considered action, start building a unity around common causes. This unity—whether visible or subliminal—is the essential factor that could turn the tide in human affairs.

THE ROAD TO PEACE

Fragrance of Peace

When life comes to its end
You, please transport
My lifeless body
Place it on the soil of Father Koubru[74]

To reduce my dead body
To cinders amidst the flames
Chopping it with axe and spade
Fills my mind with revulsion[75]

The outer cover is sure to dry out
Let it rot under the ground
Let it be of some use to future generations
Let it transform into ore in the mine

I'll spread the fragrance of peace
From Kanglei, my birthplace
In the ages to come
It will spread all over the world.

—Irom Sharmila[76]

In an era of corporate mega-giants and state irresponsibility, activists and peace scholars alike are urging the common citizen to participate actively, and take responsibility.[77] Sharmila needs no urging. She has become representative of a million ordinary people's aspirations. Standing for a world founded on dialogue and people's participation, she is encouraging others, too, to speak out fearlessly.

People want peace: the condition for leading normal lives. But peace is not an impractical concept—it is real and concrete. It requires hard work: the establishment of systems, ensuring justice at every level. A 'just peace' requires an end to violence—whether political, economic, social or psychological.

Direct violence is visible, but many enduring forms of violence are less so. Manipur suffers from various kinds of violence and conflict, involving poverty, ethnicity, territoriality and nationality, implicating insurgents, citizens and the state. The way to peace involves acknowledging the reality of these various levels of conflict, and seeking ways to transform each of them.

People of Manipur (as elsewhere) want to lead dignified lives, with clean governance, decent livelihoods, and the freedom to practise their beloved customs, speak their languages, eat their cherished foods, and worship according to diverse beliefs. They need good schools, vocational courses and colleges. Creative and highly talented people, with a civilization stretching over the millennia, want the space to preserve their heritage, and keep pace with the modern world. They want an end to violence, both direct and structural, that has eaten into their flesh and almost blotted out the possibility of peaceful and productive lives.

Peace is not quietist or defeatist: it is active and dynamic. It presupposes justice, democracy, sovereignty, basic rights and freedoms. The state, by itself, cannot ensure peace or justice. Peace will come about only when people work towards it. It can neither be imposed nor gifted: it has to be created.

Peace does not necessarily imply the absence of conflict, but rather the process set in motion when we put ourselves to the task of resolving conflict. A great deal of violence occurs when conflict is mishandled and allowed to fester, like a deep wound. Peace is in fact 'the ability to handle conflict with empathy, non-violence and creativity'.[78]

An ancient Meitei myth illustrates this possibility:

> Once upon a time there were bloody battles between gods and humans, and among different clans, with no end in sight. The goddesses intervened. They brought some things to sell to the warring groups, at a central place, and arranged a feast. When two groups ate from a common dish, a bond was established. This bond led to a settlement and durable peace.

Arambam Ongbi Memchoubi points out that women's critical role as peacemakers was recognized in various communities of Manipur.[79] Among Tangkhul Nagas, *pukhreilia* were women peacemakers, who brought an end to conflict raging between warring villages or groups. They were held in high regard. A woman who married into another village was called pukhreilia. Because she belonged to both villages, she could not be harmed in inter-village wars and conflicts. Traditionally, she worked, actively and effectively, to bring hostilities between the warring parties to an end.

ॐ

Conflict between parties who have, or think they have, incompatible goals, can be addressed in different ways.[80] Peacemakers and human rights activists such as Irom Sharmila seek to transform existing conflicts by influencing the wider social and political scenario, with the aim of transmuting the negative energy of violence into positive social and political change.

Addressing conflict within Manipuri society requires that people make space for cultural differences, acknowledge plural identities. While shared cultural traditions are strong, the differences between ethnic and cultural groups are equally real. Differences should be accepted, even celebrated as enriching. The contentious issues have to be articulated, and strategies for reconciliation worked out.

Irom Sharmila's appeal lies in the deeper layers of her personal, cultural and intellectual affiliations. She is reclaiming the right to define various dimensions of existence, political as well as personal. She asserts her allegiance to 'rationality', redefining it to make it more inclusive, rejecting the modernist version, that reduces rationality to a rarefied and rigid attribute which cannot coexist with emotion or faith. While claiming the right to universal peace and justice for all, she simultaneously claims the right to live, and die, according to particular beliefs and values.

The sources of Irom Sharmila's inspiration lie within forces that have formed her—family and community, mythology and folklore, work experiences, and her wide and varied reading. She has deep faith in her family, as the wellspring from which compassion and love develop. Ethical values get refined as the circle of empathy moves beyond family, to a whole world. Her attachment to local poetry and history affirms, rather than undercuts, her ties with wider humanity.

Her poem 'Fragrance of Peace' indicates her personal faith in Sanamahi tradition, which honours burial of the dead. She looks back to this ancient method, disowning cremation, which was imposed by Vaishnavism. Similarly, she is in favour of reintroducing the Meitei Mayek script, which went out of use due to state patronage of the Bengali language and script. At the same time, her poems are universal in intent; she wants the fragrance of peace to spread from her body even after her death, to all corners of the world.

Respect and love for one's culture can help build love for humanity, and respect for all cultures, with a conviction that each should be encouraged, its practitioners allowed freedom to keep what they want, and change what they will. There must be space to interact and understand different ways of life, appreciate and criticize, borrow and lend, so that there is fruitful growth, commingling and mutual coexistence.

The way to peace necessarily involves a committed process of dialogue, negotiation and trust building, transparency and accountability. It entails determined, conscientious action. It may not be an easy path. This is the way Irom Sharmila is illuminating. Instead of committing to it, those who want peace often despair, compromise and adapt to unacceptable situations. Sharmila's unflagging commitment has made many such people question their own apathy, and realize that they, too, can make a difference. They must grow less despondent, more hopeful, confident and articulate.

Peace requires an active engagement with conflicts, in an effort to understand and transform them. Fault lines have to be examined and attended to, not wished away. There is need to set in motion creative processes of healing and reconciliation.

Conflicts in Manipur have multiple dimensions, each requiring careful attention. The question of relations between Manipur and the rest of India, including the notion of Manipur as a sovereign state, raises thorny issues. So does the conflicted area of relations between the state's various ethnic communities. Such issues incite deep passions.

People of Manipur feel a sense of deep intimacy, love and pride in their homeland. They find a huge gap when it comes to other people, including other Indians, who seldom have any basic understanding of the conditions in Manipur. A region as rich as this finds itself marginalized in national and international arenas, blotted out in official accounts of history and culture, almost entirely missing in the national consciousness. When compounded by rampant prejudice, discriminatory treatment and even brutality meted out by a remote Centre, the result can be a potent mix of frustration, anger and a fierce turning inwards, to the sources of specific, particularistic identities.

Today, as they face a situation of acute crisis, many people turn to whatever support they can find. For Manipur, or Kangleipak as it was called before the seventeenth century, nostalgia provides some solace, helping people cope with bleak present realities. But it can also pull people back to a dead past, unable to creatively act for a better future.

Manipur is ambivalent about its location in the ongoing enterprise of fashioning India into a modern nation state. Most Manipuris accept being part of India, but with some reservations and riders. They perceive that the merger of 1949 was forced upon them, and feel alienated because they continue to be routinely treated as second-class citizens.

Most people perceive the 'Centre' as distant, and neglectful.

Several civil society and underground groups have demanded a referendum to decide on the status of Manipur—should it become a sovereign state, or remain a part of India? Insurgency has been linked to a sense of allegiance towards Manipur as a distinct entity; yet most insurgent groups today are willing to be flexible, if government brings about appropriate developmental activities.

ॐ

Identities are not 'natural'. They are the outcome of people's local practices as well as trans-local dynamics. Manipur is multicultural, with a plurality of traditions. The rest of India lacks understanding or respect for the varied communities residing here. The Indian state makes efforts to assimilate 'backward' ethnic groups as part of nation building, but this is frequently perceived as a threat, giving rise to insecurity and defensiveness. Small communities feel particularly vulnerable. They feel that their identities are in danger of being wiped out. With a small state like Manipur, even the majority ethnic group is a minority at the national level.

Contemporary ethnic conflicts in Manipur are symptomatic of a growing sense of vulnerability and insecurity. Historical understanding provides only partial answers for the current tensions; the polarization of ethnic groups is in fact a recent phenomenon. The current epidemic of violence is associated with the rise of a certain notion of modernity, and associated erosion of social customs that encouraged communities to live in harmony. Communities, and relations between communities, are being reformulated in the light of contemporary economic and political forces. Globally, land is being transformed into capital, creating vested interests and exacerbating ownership and property conflicts. Such structural dimensions of conflict call for serious rethinking of economic and political policies.[81]

Leadership of each ethnic group has marshalled distinct sets of 'facts', based on widely divergent versions of 'history', in which the 'other' is projected as exploiter, and perpetrator of violence. As identity politics gain ground, perceptions have sharpened. Peaceful methods of interaction are getting vitiated, as simmering conflicts lead to violence and riots. These processes are exacerbated by the overall ethos of a corrupt and militarized state.

Extremist insurgent groups are ideologically stagnant, advocating, at best, forms of nationalism based upon ethnic and linguistic identities, adapted to the capitalist nation state system. These underground groups are rapidly losing whatever popular support they once enjoyed. People clearly want development, not violence. But at the same time the deep emotions of hurt, injury and anger that they carry can be manipulated. In fact, all parties ultimately want an end to violence—on their own terms.

Processes of reconciliation between perceived enemies have to be consciously undertaken, acknowledging truth, exposing crimes committed (whether by any insurgent group or by the state), and setting the wheels of justice into motion. Justice must be delivered through fair, transparent and participatory methods that satisfy people on all sides. For enduring peace, justice must not only be done, but also seen and acknowledged.

To create conditions for resolving or transforming conflict, the state must alter its basic approach to development, focus on basic needs, and make a clear shift from military 'solutions' to political engagement. For a people living under siege, there is nothing more precious than the possibility of normal life, peace and justice. Irrespective of community affiliations, most people in Manipur today would strongly support an authentic peace process. Of course, reconciliation between hostile parties will require mediation and negotiation; it will not happen automatically or magically.

Militarization is certainly not leading to peace; indeed it is eroding the very possibility of peace. Repression cannot resolve Manipur's problems. By unleashing AFSPA upon the people, insurgency has spiralled upwards, spinning out of control. Cycles of violence have been generated in Manipur, with insurgent militias and the state's armed forces locked in fruitless combat. Civilians are the main losers.

ॐ

The Indian government did not criticize brutal assault on peaceful protesters in neighbouring Myanmar, in October 2007. Several countries registered protest at the extreme violence of the Myanmarese junta government, but India prevaricated. The reason was clear—India's militarized state needs Myanmar's support to crush insurgency across the long, shared borders. The two states cooperate because they have similar 'strategic interests', and share, though perhaps to different degrees, similar repressive anti-people strategies.

Dissenters are being labelled 'criminals'. In one sweeping brushstroke, entire groups of people (whether ethnic groups or political sects) are being criminalized. Peace is hardly possible in a scenario where the state delegitimizes dissent, and resorts to militarization as the means to deal with people's grievances. As both insurgents and the state pile up, and increasingly use, arms and ammunition, *their methods have become indistinguishable*. Revenge is confused with righteous action, justice with injustice, and peace with war. In this murky atmosphere, nobody wins, and peace grows distant.

Merely trying to 'flush out' the underground groups will not succeed. Insurgents and the militaristic state are today hardened and recalcitrant, distorted mirror images of one another. Logically, violence cannot show a way out of violence. State terrorism will not end insurgents' terrorism.

Irom Sharmila, along with ordinary citizens of Manipur, insists that a different way is possible—a way to move out of the trap of violence. It is a way of principled dissent and unwavering resistance, as well as active engagement in dialogue, reconciliation and just actions. Choosing this way will help to create a different ethos, with hope and goodwill as building blocks, rather than hate and revenge.

Some issues raised by underground groups call for long-term, sustained dialogue between parties. Government should invite insurgent groups to dialogue, and demonstrate enduring commitment to evolving peaceful solutions. In the case of hardened and ruthless militants, search operations should be meticulously conducted, and judicial procedures duly followed, with full transparency and accountability from armed forces and the police.

Counter-insurgency must connect with popular aspirations. Developmental activities ensuring food security, employment, health care, educational inputs and agricultural revival have to be an integral part of the process. The purpose of counter-insurgency should be clear and visible: peace in the region, enabling pursuit of development in consonance with people's needs and cultures. Irom Sharmila, along with several civil society groups and individuals, is demanding not just an end to AFSPA, but basically a genuine response to people's grievances, and an authentic process of development.

The state and insurgent groups have yet to take the critical decision of turning towards peace. Multiple conflicts can be resolved if there is clear intention and strategic action.

౭

R.K. Randhoni Devi, joint secretary of Poirei Leimarol Meira Paibi Apunba, says, 'The main ideology of the Meira Paibis is to bring peace in the state. We will continue fighting ...' Activist Elangbam Bimola Devi explains, 'We have been playing a vital role in order to bring unity among the various communities in Manipur.' Taruni Devi muses, 'Generally it is the poor people who are the saviours of Manipur. They work harder in order to safeguard the integrity of Manipur; rich people hardly join our ranks.'[82]

Larik Yumnam, president of Kangleipak Lamjing Apunba Meira Lup, says women will do anything to save the integrity of the state. During Kuki–Naga, Meitei–Pangal and Paite–Kuki clashes, her organization played a vital role in restoring peace and harmony in the state. It played a similar role during the anti-ceasefire agitation of 2001, helping contain tensions between Naga and other ethnic groups of the state.

At a seminar held by the National Campaign Committee against Militarisation and for Repeal of AFSPA, Dr Dhanabir Laishram of All Manipur Unity Committee (AMUCO) noted, 'We need to change the mentality and come to a common understanding. We should hold workshops and training programs to build an understanding of peace.' Joseph Hmar of All Tribal Students' Union of Manipur (ATSUM) stressed the importance of bringing all stakeholders together on a common platform. Robert T. Maram of the All Naga Students' Union of Manipur (ANSUM) voiced agreement, saying this was essential in order to move forward to a common solution. Babloo Loitongbam, HRA, noted, 'The kind of relation indigenous communities have with their land is very different from the way it is in industrial societies ... Different communities have common interests in Manipur. I may be born Meitei but the Naga brothers are our brothers ... We must take charge of the peace process. We must not let the process rule us.'[83]

North East Network (NEN) held a 'Citizens' Roundtable on Manipur and Beyond', in November 2004, to facilitate constructive dialogue between activists of different hues.[84] Among the delegates were K. Maharabi Singh of All Manipur NGO Forum; Mangshi Haokip, president of Kuki Mothers Association; Sitara Begum, president of All Manipur Muslim Women's Organization; Valleyrose Hungyo of the Naga Women's Union of Manipur; and Basanta Kumar Wareppa of Amnesty International. Several participants noted that women frequently face security forces and underground groups, yet are never included in conflict resolution processes. They articulated a need for stronger networking between grassroot organizations, in order to take micro-struggles to the macro level. To resolve the Manipur crisis, they suggested the focus should be on political measures, judicial remedies and repeal of AFSPA. Peace talks should be held, and civil society organizations must lobby with underground groups to prevent aggressive actions. An independent body of experts should identify long-term measures to restore peace and prosperity through employment generation, development of local resources, appropriate technologies, education, training and health care.

A meeting on AFSPA was held by the Control Arms Foundation of India, New Delhi, in May 2008, convened by Ms Binalakshmi Nepram. The meeting brought together a number of young people from Manipur, Nagaland, Sikkim and Delhi, to strategize for repeal of the Act. Ms Soibam Haripriya shared the history of AFSPA, describing it as a colonial legacy. Ms Neikesanuo Sorhie from the Naga People's Movement for Human Rights shared the status of AFSPA in Nagaland, where in spite of ceasefire, killings still take place. Lawyer Mr Baban Prakash explained that the Act fundamentally violates the Constitution of India.

In November 2007, the People's Initiative for Peace in Manipur (PIPM), a coalition of civil society organizations from Manipur and other parts of India, brought out a declaration for peace in Manipur. PIPM, which includes members from different ethnic groups, launched the peace declaration in Imphal. Over 600 people attended the launch. Academics, representatives of popular organizations and religious leaders supported the declaration, which focuses on people's participation in the peace process. PIPM's strategy is to raise awareness within the country and enlist the support of common citizens, political actors and civil society organizations, so that they all participate in a movement for peace. To pursue this quest, PIPM organized a round table on the issues of Manipur in April 2008, in Delhi. The meeting was well attended, with inputs from Mr Nobo Kishore of PIPM, Dr Bimola Devi, head of political science department, Imphal University, students and representatives of civil society organizations such as The Other Media, and IPAC-Delhi. A core group was formed to take the process forward. Such efforts by civil society groups have continued over the next years.

Clearly, many people in Manipur are sensing an urgent need to actively participate in decision-making processes, rather than leaving matters in the hands of remote bureaucrats and politicians. They are voicing an urgent need to end violence, and discussing possible ways to restore order in Manipur. People's keenness to participate in the polity is a very positive feature of the present scenario.

A mature leadership is required, with understanding and ability to transform existing crises in non-violent ways. Extremist insurgent groups have lost popular support, and are ideologically stagnant. Some moderate insurgent groups are willing to negotiate and arrive at reasonable solutions. Potential to bring about radical change lies in ordinary peace-loving citizens, and the numerous civil society groups, human rights, youth and women's organizations. The diverse strands need to be strengthened by coming together and weaving a new tapestry, creating a vibrant, transformative politics.

MILES TO GO

People's movements against violence, with women at the forefront, continue to be a force to reckon with. Have these struggles yielded any concrete results? One very visible success is, what is called by ordinary Manipuris, 'the liberation of Kangla'.

A Victory: the Liberation of Kangla Fort

Union Minister of State for Home, Sriprakash Jaiswal, promised to vacate the historic Kangla Fort by December 31, 2004. The Fort was captured by the British in 1891 and has been with the Indian Army since Independence. It has been a bone of contention. Should the promise be kept, Manorama's death will mark a turning point in the history of Manipur.

—'The Merciless Killing of Thangjam Manorama', worldpress.org, 23 July 2004[85]

The capture of Kangla Fort by the British in 1891 marked the highest humiliation and disgrace; its continued occupation by Indian armed forces has been a festering wound in the heart of Manipur. Throughout the twentieth century, people of the state raised their voices for the liberation of this site. The demand for liberation of Kangla has been implicit in Irom Sharmila's protest, and in the Meira Paibi struggles. Because of these protests, and the popular support and media attention they received, particularly after the July 2004 anti-rape agitation, the government realized it should accede to at least some of the demands being raised. The Union home minister promised to vacate Kangla Fort, in which battalions of the 17th Assam Rifles were stationed, by end-2004; conduct an enquiry into the Thangjam Manorama rape-and-murder case; and set up a high-level committee for review of AFSPA.

On 20 November 2004, the government actually withdrew the 17th Assam Rifles from Kangla Fort. For the first time in 113 years, common people could now freely enter the Kangla Fort area, walk around in what remains of the ancient palace compounds, shrines, sacred waterbodies, underground chambers and tunnels. Kangla Fort symbolizes Manipur's heritage—political, cultural and philosophical, and is tied up with people's deepest aspirations.

The liberation of Kangla would not have happened but for spirited protests by Meira Paibis, Irom Sharmila, and other civil society organizations and citizens. The move marked a significant victory, indicating that the state *does* respond to popular aspirations and non-violent people's struggles.

Assam Rifles, a paramilitary force controlled by the Indian home ministry and army, is the main security force in Manipur, and is majorly responsible for enforcing AFSPA. The force was originally created by the British colonial regime in the nineteenth century, to quell popular rebellion in the North-East. It has been greatly expanded since 1947, and now numbers some forty battalions.

Removal of Assam Rifles from Kangla was a morale booster for the people of Manipur. For the government, it was a conciliatory move, in recognition of popular anger occasioned by rampant abuse of power by the security forces. The state was bewildered and confused, pressured by diverse compulsions. It felt that some concessions ought to be made to the people's movement. However, it had no intention to stick to all the promises made by Jaiswal.

In 2004, Chief Minister Ibobi Singh proposed the lifting of AFSPA from Imphal. The Congress-led United Progressive Alliance Central government announced an order lifting AFSPA from Imphal. But the military high command strongly objected to relaxation of AFSPA anywhere in Manipur. Chief of Army Staff N.C.Vij and other senior military officers communicated to the home minister that the order lifting AFSPA in Imphal compromises security. They expressed their concern that the government's concession to anti-AFSPA agitation in Manipur could lead to similar movements elsewhere in the North-East, and in Jammu and Kashmir. However, AFSPA was withdrawn from the municipal limits of Imphal.

Following up the other promises made by Jaiswal in July 2004 in response to popular agitation, the Manipur state government set up an enquiry commission to examine the circumstances surrounding the death of Thangjam Manorama. Assam Rifles refused to cooperate with the enquiry commission: the accused personnel repeatedly ignored orders to testify. Assam Rifles failed to even confirm which personnel were on duty at the time. Culpability could not, therefore, be established. Guwahati High Court ruled that the Manipur government had no authority to prosecute the central armed forces, under the provisions of AFSPA. Thus, no due judicial process took place. The case was reopened in 2010, and still no one was held responsible for the killing of Thangjam Manorama.

The Central government appointed the Justice Jeevan

Reddy Committee to review AFSPA, in 2004. The Committee submitted its report the following year, recommending that the Act be withdrawn. The government refused to make the report public. After media located and publicized the full text of the report, the government still refused to act on it. The Committee recommended that AFSPA should be withdrawn, pointing out that the Act, 'for whatever reason, has become a symbol of oppression, an object of hate and an instrument of discrimination and high-handedness'. Ten years down the line, the report has still not been officially tabled in Parliament. In effect, the government is categorically refusing to accept, or even acknowledge, the report—of a Committee it itself set up. Due democratic procedures have been thrown to the winds.

Soon after the Meira Paibis protested against the Thangjam Manorama rape-cum-murder, they formed a broad-based forum, the Apunba Manipur Kanba Ima Lup or 'Mothers' Association to Save Manipur'. This forum continues to actively struggle for repeal of AFSPA.

One significant concession by the state, to popular struggles, has been the liberation of Kangla. This milestone victory has repercussions on people's consciousness, far deeper than is immediately evident.

Kangla is revered as the most sacred spot in Manipur. It means, literally, 'dry land', and is envisioned as the first land to have emerged from the primordial waters that once covered the earth. Imphal Valley, earlier submerged in water, gradually became habitable as the waters receded. Kangla is integral to Manipur's mythology and history. It is pictured in sacred cosmology as the navel of the world, the first organ fashioned by the gods when they created Earth. In the collective subconscious, the entire land is patterned like a human body, with different spots representing specific organs, each marked by a symbolic temple or sacred building. When Assam Rifles vacated Kangla Fort in November 2004, a local journalist, Oinam Anand, represented popular sentiment by writing, 'We now have Kangla, the navel where our umbilical cord meets our mother Manipur ...'[86]

Kangla has been inscribed in the collective imagination as the fount of political power, since Ningthoujou Pakhangba established it as his capital in AD 33. Successive kings ruled from this site, rendering it the centre of power in Manipur. King Khagemba (1597–1652) started constructing a huge mud wall around the entire fort, with a perimeter of about four miles; King Khunjaoba (1652–66) continued building this enclosure, and King Paikhomba completed it. The coronation palace and the sacred Kangla Sha—two gigantic stone dragons—were built during the reign of King Chourajit (1803–13). Burmese invaders destroyed a few historical buildings during the Seven Years Devastation (1819–26), and the British destroyed several more architectural marvels.

After capturing Kangla on 27 November 1891, the British noticed blood stains in the mouths of the Kangla Sha, and took it to be the blood of British officers whom Manipuris had beheaded. As revenge and punishment, they blasted the dragons into pieces. They occupied Kangla, and shut the entire premises off from the public. After Manipur's merger with India, the Indian security forces occupied the place due to its strategic importance. In 1950, Assam Rifles battalions were housed inside Kangla Fort. Civilian population was barred from entering any part of the extensive Kangla premises.

Removing the security personnel and lifting prohibition on public entry have been a long-standing demand of the Manipuri people. Successive governments promised to shift Assam Rifles from Kangla, but failed to do so. It was the powerful popular protests since the year 2000 that 'rung the bells of alarm in the ears of the Central Government, they realized the sentiments and anguish of the people of Manipur, and Assam Rifles had no other option but to call it a day after their long occupation of the Fort for over 50 years.'[87]

On 20 November 2004, the Director General, Assam Rifles, handed over the key of Kangla Fort to the chief minister, in the presence of the Indian prime minister. This has gone down as a red-letter day in the history of Manipur, a day of restoration, on which a long-cherished dream of Manipuris was fulfilled.

The tall, carved gates of Kangla Fort, in front of which countless popular protests have been held, are now opened to the public. Kangla belongs, once again, to the people of Manipur. The state government proposes to renovate and reconstruct the coronation hall and palaces, the mud wall fencing all around, the altars to Koubru, Wangbren and Thumjao Lairembi, Govindjee and other temples, and plant a botanical garden where rare medicinal plants will be preserved.

People of Manipur have formed citizens' committees which, with aid from government agencies and NGOs, are excavating ruins of palaces, temples and other important sites within Kangla. The citizens' committees have already rebuilt the Kangla Sha. The two majestic dragons greet us proudly, as we enter Kangla Fort in mid-2007. People from all over Manipur come here to explore Kangla, and worship at its various shrines. Irom Singhjit and his daughter Sunibala spend a few minutes in worship at one of the shrines; then he points out ruined palaces whose underground chambers are being excavated, a sacred pool, the Govindjee temple, and relates various legends and historical facts associated with these.

The restoration of Kangla is replete with political significance, and resonates at deeper levels of cosmic and historical memory. Perhaps the restoration of Kangla Fort signifies the beginning of the creation of a new world—a world made, this time, by the will of millions of ordinary people. In their more hopeful moments, this is what the people of Manipur feel.

☛

Yet, as we know, all is not well in the state of Manipur. In September 2004, journalist Kranti Kumar noted, 'The state of Manipur was declared disturbed in 1980, and during the subsequent quarter century, Indian security forces have repeatedly committed human rights violations and brutal atrocities.'[88] Such atrocities have not stopped, AFSPA has not been withdrawn, and Irom Sharmila has not broken her protest fast.

Members of Asian Human Rights Commission, Hong Kong, the foremost Asian human rights body, have investigated atrocities in Manipur, that are taking place with impunity even now, due to the special powers granted to the armed forces personnel. Bijo Francis of AHRC has provided detailed documentation of some victim testimonies in Moreh and Thoubal areas.[89] This documentation gives an idea of the ground realities for very ordinary people of the state, who live in fear of arbitrary assaults both by underground groups and by the armed forces.

On 17 July 2006, twenty-eight-year-old Namoijam Chotoi of Thoubal was arrested, arbitrarily, detained and tortured. His father, Bibison, a poor farmer, said that Indian army men knocked at their door, kicked it down, stormed in and held a rifle to his head. They pulled Chotoi out from bed. A few weeks earlier, an underground group had abducted and assaulted Chotoi and he had injuries and bandages on his body. Yet, army men beat and dragged him into their vehicle. Bibison next met Chotoi on 25 July at the court of the chief judicial magistrate, Bishnupur. Chotoi had been tortured in spite of his unhealed old wounds, and had gone deaf due to severe beating. Bibison sold the paddy stored for the whole year and pawned whatever gold they had, to raise Rs 11,000 as lawyers' fees. Personnel at Moirang police station also extorted money from Bibison.

Huirem Bhakta was picked up by the CRPF on 17 July 2006, from his house in Thoubal. He too had been abducted and beaten up by an underground group. CRPF personnel took him to their camp and grilled him as to whether he possessed guns, grenades and wireless sets. When they realized he did not, they demanded information on who did. But Bhakta did not know. They tied his hands and legs, held him down with an iron rod, forced his mouth open with a rifle barrel, inserted a stone into his mouth and kept beating him. Later they took him to the regular police, who refused to take him in, scared that he might die of his injuries. Bhakta had to pay the police Rs 2,500 before they would take him from the CRPF. He had to pay a lawyer Rs 11,500 for bailing him out. On the night of his arrest, CRPF handed over an arrest memo to his relatives. He asks, 'What is the purpose of such a piece of paper if they ignore all laws and torture us at will? I have filed a complaint with the superintendent of police but I am sure there will be no action taken on it. The CRPF is more powerful than anyone in the government.'

Moirangthem Leibaklai, mother of thirty-year-old Moirangthem Ibohal, asks simply, 'What is an arrest memo? A document to measure the level of torture?' She speaks from bitter experience. On the night of 30 June 2006, army personnel stormed in and began searching her house in Moreh. They beat Ibohal brutally, while his wife and three children protested, forced the family to sign a paper at gunpoint saying that Ibohal was associated with UNLF, and then dragged him away. Leibaklai and Ibohal's wife went with neighbours to the police station, but were not allowed to meet him. A police officer told them that if the army had given an arrest memo, they would not torture him much! Next day the army produced her son. Leibaklai recalls, 'I was like a piece of wood. The son to whom I had given birth and brought up and who was to take care of me and his family was so brutally injured he could not even open his eyes. His face was swollen and he was so red from bruises that it was the worst sight I have ever seen ...You cannot understand this pain unless you are a mother. Look around you and every mother in this place will have a similar story to tell ... What kind of justice system do we have in this country?' After twelve days, the police produced Ibohal in court. When Leibaklai came out of court an army officer threatened to burn down her house and rape the women if they complained again. She adds, 'I am no more afraid. I am sure that by the time my son is released he will have suffered so much that he will find it difficult to lead a normal life ...'

On the same night as Ibohal's arrest, twenty-six-year-old Priyokumar, thirty-five-year-old Brojen Thoigam, and twenty-one-year-old N. Boinao were picked up, and subjected to arbitrary detention and torture. Priyokumar's wife Sobitha alleges her husband, a daily-wage labourer, was tortured in army custody: a wire tied to his penis, and connected to a power supply. He was released on 21 July, but lives in fear that the army will come for him again. Hemanta Ithobi Thoigam, Brojen Thoigam's mother, says, 'It was horrible to see young men being treated this way by the forces that came supposedly to protect us from criminals and anti-national forces.'

Jayantha, Boinao's grandfather, says soldiers had brought a policeman with them, Abdul Wahid, who bravely refused to file false charges. Wahid, police constable at Moreh police station, confirms this, saying the army men asked him to sign memos claiming that five 9mm cartridges were seized from Boinao, and a Chinese-made grenade from another person, but he refused to sign the fabricated documents. Wahid concludes, 'The army appears to be making up cases with which to charge people with crimes to justify their operations.' He adds that police, magistrates and doctors are afraid of the army; so one can only imagine how afraid the ordinary person must be.

Mani Thombi, mother of Jano, a mentally and physically

disabled young man, reports that about 100 soldiers surrounded their house in Moreh, past midnight on 16 July 2006. They searched the house, but found nothing incriminating. Yet they kicked Jano into their vehicle and took him away; he was crying with fear. Thombi informed local women activists, and they gathered at the police station the next morning. Her son had a haunted look in his eyes because he had been brutally tortured. She asks, 'To whom shall we complain about all this? The police are equally helpless. To the army or to the government who sent the army here? Or to the insurgents? Every day here is uncertain. You can never be sure about tomorrow.'

On 21 July 2006, around midnight 24th Assam Rifles personnel illegally arrested twenty-three-year-old Soibam Mithun of Moreh. Mithun testifies he was blindfolded, beaten on the head with a rifle butt, and tortured by electric shocks applied to his testicles. He was pressured to say he was a UNLF cadre. When he said he is not connected with any organization and makes his living by giving private tuitions, they hit him and applied electric shocks. Some others were being tortured in the same room in a similar manner. After being released, Mithun refuses to step out of his house since he is terrified of soldiers, and there are soldiers everywhere. He despairs, 'I do not think I can live here anymore. I do not know what to do now. I want to finish my life.'

☥

These are just a few examples of abuse of human rights, in Manipur today. Impartial journalists observe that the impunity enjoyed by the state security forces has made them 'essentially function as a terrorist state-sponsored gang. Over the decades, they have committed murders and rapes, destroyed dwellings, subjected people to arbitrary arrests, and humiliated people.'[90]

When a sensitive young citizen refuses to countenance these methods, the state denounces her as a criminal. Irom Sharmila says, 'I want to be a symbol of justice.' And to many people, that is exactly what she is. She has become a symbol of the popular will for peace and justice. People have an abiding respect for her, close to reverence, and a careful affection. They recognize in Irom Sharmila the possibility of actually building a different reality.

If one person can give up so much for her beliefs, there must be some substance to her struggle, some hope that the world will change. She has become that ray of hope, a living possibility of transformation. Basking in the warmth of that golden glow, we can let our fears melt, feel the spark in our hearts, and allow ourselves to join, and further create, the current for change!

Around the focal point of Sharmila's fasting figure, ways to dialogue and a consensus towards peace might well emerge. She has never been a rabble-rouser or a fighter of elections. For years, she has been locked away, in an effort to break her will, and the will of all those who struggle for peace and justice. Despite forced physical isolation, she remains a leader. She leads by sheer example. Through her daily life, she proves that the human spirit will never stop aspiring for peace, dreaming of justice and courageously sacrificing for the highest good. Even in the worst of times, somebody will stand up and speak the truth, somebody will make a difference.

The 'difference' is an inspiration and stimulation, for all of us to reflect and re-examine what we believe in, what we

live by. Are we living in bubble-worlds, enveloped in false
sheaths of security? Why do we allow faceless states to take
over our lives, to take decisions on our behalf—decisions over
our life and death? We are frightened, understandably so, by
the escalating levels of terrorist violence in the world. But
so long as we do not see that state violence, in the name of
'counter-terrorism', is not the solution, we remain caught up
in a false sense of security. We give up our power to the state,
which works on the same logic of violence as the terrorists.
We need a different way—we need to find this way together
with all the others, for it is a matter of the gravest concern
for the human race. By silent apathy, we acquiesce to the
violence raging around us. If we want peace and justice in
our lives, and in the world, the time to express our choice
is—*right now.*

EPILOGUE: INSIDE THE LABYRINTH

One April evening in Imphal—it could be 2008 or 2009 . . . or 2013 or 2014—Lai Haraoba, the sacred dance is approaching its final hour. A dancer announces that nobody should leave in between the movements that are to follow. A person can either leave immediately, or else afterwards. I stay of course.

Rhythmic music accompanies the movements—the sonorous beating of drums, and a Maiba playing haunting notes on his pena, flute. A Maibi drives evil spirits away from the stage, using her double-edged knife for protection.

Maibis, elderly priestesses, beautiful in red and white, lead the ritual dance, and other dancers follow, swaying sinuously. They make serpentine movements, gracefully weaving their way in intricate patterns. An aerial view would be ideal, for then one could see the patterns being painted on the ground, clear brushstrokes, swirling lines, like magic calligraphy. It takes years to learn this dance, and one wrong step can mean cosmic imbalance.

The serpentine movements symbolize Pakhangba, the dragon-headed divine serpent-protector of the external world, the public sphere. Dancers trace the path of the serpent's coils, a mystical labyrinth. These movements are designed to protect all those present from harmful influences, for another year.91 Human action, when in consonance with the divine, keeps the world in balance.

The dance requires total concentration, from the dancers, and the viewers. Anybody leaving in the midst of the dance would break the magic. It would bring catastrophe into human affairs.

In a way, Irom Sharmila's fast is like a dance, which began years ago. She is imprisoned, physically islolated, and force-fed. And yet, we can imagine her engaged in the slow, sure movements of a dance—a salutation to divine forces. She will not leave midway. It is as if she is deep within a labyrinth, weaving her way in measured steps. It is an exacting dance, testing the limits of human endurance. It is an inspired dance, led by the vision of a radically changed world. The rest of us, co-dancers or 'viewers', are vitally important too. In just the viewing, we have become witnesses, part of a totality we barely comprehend. We too cannot abandon the dance midway. We cannot leave. Not yet ... not just yet.

Nobody knows where it will end, or when. The end is not in Irom Sharmila's hands. In her hands is only the intention, the discipline and the art. To this, she is dedicated: it is her vocation. Her moves are creating their own rhythm, ushering a certain order into the world. Like Sharmila, we too have begun listening to a different music, powerful and resonant.

Through her dance, which has some of the qualities of a trance, she hopes to make a difference to the human world, bringing it into closer harmony with the divine order. The manifest world is in immense disorder, but the process of making peace is also going on: invisibly. We sense it sometimes, in silence and in solitude, in the collective aspiration of a spiritual gathering, or in the marvellous unity of a people's movement.

When the change manifests, the violence will abate. She will take the final steps, and retreat backstage, to rest awhile. People will offer fruit and sweets to the gods, in reverence and gratitude. The Maibis will distribute these to each person present: Sharmila too will savour the taste.

NOTES

1. Deepti Priya Mehrotra, *A Passion for Freedom: The Story of Kisanin Jaggi Devi* (New Delhi: IGNCA, 2005).

2. N. Vijay Lakshmi, 'A Woman's Fast to Protest Abuses by the Army', *PUCL Bulletin*, <http://www.pucl.org/reports/Manipur/2001/sharmila.htm>, posted on 18 September 2002.

3. Bhabananda Takhellambum, *Women's Uprising in Manipur: A Legacy Continued* (New Delhi: WISCOMP, 2003).

4. Chunkham Sheelaramani, 'Gender Construction in the Meitei Society', *Quarterly Journal 23, Manipuri Women on A New Role*, February 2007, p 34–44. Published by Manipur State Kala Akademi at Imphal.

5. Naorem Sanajaoba, ed., *Manipur Past and Present—The Ordeals and Heritage of a Civilisation, Vol. 2: Philosophy, Culture and Literature* (New Delhi: Mittal, 1991).

6. Aung San Suu Kyi, *Let's Visit Burma* (London: Burke,1985), p 34, cited in Arambam Ongbi Memchoubi, 'The Indigenous Meitei Women', *Quarterly Journal*, ibid., p 1–18.

7. Gangumumei Kabui, *History of Manipur, Vol. 1: Pre-Colonial Period* (New Delhi: National Publishing House, 1991), p 289.

8. Manjusri Chaki-Sircar, *Feminism in a Traditional Society* (New Delhi: Shakti Books, 1984), p 26.

9. Bimola Devi, 'The Changing Role of Manipuri Women', *Quarterly Journal*, ibid., p 19–31.

10. When Jawaharlal Nehru visited Shillong in 1937, he met Gaidinlieu in jail and gave her the title 'Rani'. She was imprisoned up to 1947, but even the Indian government did

not permit her return to Manipur. She was awarded a pension and kept in Mokokchung, Nagaland. Belatedly, in 1972, she was awarded a freedom fighter award, and in 1987 a Padma Bhushan.

11. Arambam Ongbi Memchoubi, *Quarterly Journal*, ibid., p 11.

12. Ramani Devi, in Gunjan Veda, ed., *Tailoring Peace: The Citizens' Roundtable on Manipur and Beyond* (Guwahati: North-East Network, 2005), p 32–33.

13. Interview with Ima Taruni Devi, by Deepti Priya Mehrotra on 19 April 2007 in Imphal.

14. Taruni Devi, in Gunjan Veda, ibid., p 33–34.

15. Valleyrose Hungyo, in Gunjan Veda, ibid., p 45.

16. Yamini Devi, 'Ningol Chaukoba' in *Parvat ke Paar*, a collection of short stories, translated from Manipuri to Hindi by Elaibam Vijaylakshmi (Imphal: Rai Praveena Brothers, 2005), p 131–138. See also 'Satvoplabdhi', p 74–77; 'Kala Bazar', p 117–120; 'Sakshar', p 111–116; and 'Chaobi Mausi ka Pension', p 149–156.

17. Yamini Devi, ibid., 'Jandhvi', p 105–110; 'Kamaoo Patni', p 91–95.

18. Yamini Devi, ibid., 'Sushila ka Bhagya', p 55–61.

19. Chunkham Sheelaramani, *Quarterly Journal*, ibid.

20. Gunjan Veda, ibid., p 38.

21. Press Information Bureau, Defence Wing, 'Annual Report—Army in the Northeast', from e-pao.net, webcast on 16 November 2006.

22. E.N. Rammohan, *Insurgent Frontiers: Essays from the Troubled Northeast* (New Delhi: India Research Press, 2005), p 124–127 and 166–176.

23. Naorem Sanajaoba, 'The Armed Forces (Special Powers) Act: An Unproclaimed Emergency and Gross Injustice', in *Article 2 of the International Covenant on Civil and Political Rights, Special edition on Militarisation and Impunity in Manipur*, Vol. 5, No. 6, December 2006, p 29–34.

24. Kranti Kumar, 'India: Popular Agitation Against Army Atrocities Engulfs the Northeast State of Manipur', *World Socialist Website*, 15 September 2004.

25. Justic Fazal Ali is quoted in Khangembam Chonjohn, 'The Armed Forces (Special Powers) Act: "Procedure Established by Law"?' in *Article 2*, ibid., p 35–37.

26. 'The Meaning of Article 2: Implementation of Human Rights', in *Article 2*, ibid., front and back covers.

27. O. Kulabidhu Singh, *Sharmila: A Mission of Peace* (Imphal: Oinam Ongbi Gulabmachu Devi, 2006), p 46–66, citing Ranjit Singh, *Unrest in Manipur*, L. Ibomcha, *Manipur under AFSPA*; Committee on Human Rights (CoHR) and Human Rights Alert (HRA).

28. O. Kulabidhu Singh, ibid.

29. Economic and Social Council, UNESCO, *Report of Commission on Human Rights, Fifty-ninth Session*, 2003.

30. Irom Sharmila, 7 November 2006, AIIMS, New Delhi.

31. Interview with Ajita, by Marc-Olivier Parlatano in 'Manipur, a Land of Coveted Strategical Resources', *Le Courrier*, Switzerland, 13 April 2007.

32. Interview with Seram Rojesh, 22 April 2007, Imphal.

33. N. Vijayalakshmi Brara, *A Situational Analysis of Women and Girls in Manipur* (New Delhi: National Commission of Women, 2005), p 20. Table 2.3 indicates that between 1981 and 1991, the number of female main workers in cultivation rose from 152,759 to 194,232; in agricultural labour from 17,652 to 28,199; in trade and commerce from 8,934 to 9,831; comparable figures for male cultivators is from 211,862 to 243,267; for male agricultural labourers from 10,961 to 17,652; and for men in trade and commerce from 10,402 to 17,352. See also Tables 2.4, 2.5 and 2.6. From Table 2, we see that Manipur's female workforce participation rate is 40.51, which is the third highest among the states and Union territories. Above it are only Mizoram and Himachal Pradesh. Table 2.11 indicates that in the hill districts of Senapati and Churachandpur there are 2,532 and 5,395 women respectively in household industries; the comparable figures for men are 924 and 1,646. Similarly, in the valley districts of Bishnupur and Thoubal, there are 9,238 and 16,449 women in household industry respectively; comparable figures for men are 2,157 and 3,744.

34. N. Vijayalakshmi Brara, ibid. The total population of Manipur recorded in 2001 Census of India is 2,293,896.

35. N, Vijayalakshmi Brara, ibid.

36. See Note 22.

37. Monideepa Choudhuri, 'Manipur Resists Land Alienation', *Infochange India News and Features*, May 2008.

38. Press release by Citizens' Concern for Dams and Development, Manipur, 7 July 2007.

39. Anuradha Chenoy, 'Militarisation, Conflict and Women in South Asia', Lois Lorentzen and Jennifer Turpin, ed., *Women and War Reader* (New York University Press, 1998), p 101–110.

40. See Note 27.

41. Verbal communication, Shri Kotishwar Singh, senior advocate, Imphal.

42. Ng. Ibodon, 'Manipuri Women Today: A Conversation', *Quarterly Journal*, ibid., p 95–104.

43. Teresa Rehman, 'Who is Ima Gyaneswari?', *Infochange Agenda: Reporting Conflict*, Issue 14, 2009, p 32–33.

44. Gunjan Veda, ibid. p 33–34.

45. Khelen Thokchom, 'She Stoops to Conquer', *The Telegraph*, 25 July 2004, cited in Khelena Gurumayum, *The Role of Manipuri Women in Crisis Management during the Extension of Ceasefire between the Government of India and NSCN-IM without Territorial Limits* (New Delhi: WISCOMP, 2007), p 40.

46. Lisa Schirch, *Ritual and Symbol in Peacebuilding* (Bloomfield: Kumarian Press, 2005), has an interesting discussion on the use and importance of symbolic and ritual action by peacebuilders.

47. Gene Sharp, *There Are Realistic Alternatives* (Boston: Albert Einstein Institute, 2003), p 39–48.

48. Irom Sharmila interviewed by Kavita Joshi, September 2005. Quoted by Kavita Joshi, 'My Fasting is a Means; I Have No Other', *Infochange India News and Features*, November 2006.

49. Thomas Pantham, 'Post-Relativism in Emancipatory Thought: Gandhi's Swaraj and Satyagraha', D.L. Sheth and Ashish Nandy, ed., *The Multiverse of Democracy* (New Delhi: Sage, 1996), p 210–229.

NOTES 213

50. L.M. Bhole, 'The Gandhian Model of Nonviolent Social Order', in Mahendra Kumar, ed., *Nonviolence: Contemporary Issues and Challenges* (New Delhi: Gandhi Peace Foundation, 1994), p 273–283.

51. Lokendra Arambam, 'Manipur—A Ritual Theatre State', in Naorem Sanajaoba, ibid., p 57–75.

52. M.K. Gandhi, 'A Talk on Non-violence', *Harijan*, 14 March 1936, in M.K. Gandhi, *Non-violence in Peace and War*, (Ahmedabad: Navajivan Publishing House, 1942), p 154–157.

53. Henry David Thoreau, cited in J.B. Kripalani, 'Civil Disobedience', in S. Mukherjee and S. Ramaswamy, ed., *Facets of Mahatma Gandhi, Vol. I: Non-violence and Satyagraha* (New Delhi: Deep and Deep, 1994), p 63–73.

54. Aung San Suu Kyi, 'May We Go Forward in Disciplined Strength', speech delivered on 10 February 1995.

55. M.K. Gandhi, 'Theory and Practice of Non-violence', *Young India*, 31 December 1931, in M.K. Gandhi, *Non-violence in Peace and War*, ibid., p 148–153.

56. Original is in Manipuri; Hindi translation given personally by Irom Sharmila to Deepti Priya Mehrotra, who translated it into English.

57. India Social Forum documents and papers, December 2006.

58. Kanglei is the short form of Kangleipak, one of the archaic names of Manipur.

59. Irom Sharmila, *Quarterly Journal*, ibid., p 92, translated by Tayenjam Bijoykumar Singh.

60. N. Vijay Lakshmi, ibid.

61. 'In Support of Irom Sharmila Chanu', *PUCL Bulletin*, November 2006.

62. Binayak Sen was helping to document and build public opinion regarding cases of human rights violations by Salwa Judum in Chhattisgarh. The Salwa Judum is an armed force set up by the state, ostensibly to contain Naxalite violence in Chhattisgarh, but in fact unleashing a reign of terror on the local citizens.

63. Reproduced in e-pao.net, webcast on 10 July 2007, courtesy *The Sangai Express*.

64. Yamini Devi, ibid.,'Combing Operation', p 121–126; and 'Dadi Ma ki Peruk Kangsu', p 127–130.

65. Ashish Chandra, *Human Rights and Conflict Resolution* (New Delhi: Rajat Publications, 2000).

66. 'Protest demonstrations against AFSPA in six nations begin', *Imphal Free Press*, 13 September 2007; K. Anurag, 'Support Pours for Manipur's Fasting Activist Sharmila', *UNI*, 13 September 2007; 'Army Act Protest Goes Global', *The Telegraph*,13 September 2007, and 'NAPM, Parivar Pay Respect to Sharmila', *The Sangai Express*, 16 September 2007.

67. B.B. Sharma, in Gunjan Veda, ibid., p 18.

68. Thomas Weber, *Gandhi, Gandhism and the Gandhians* (New Delhi: Roli, 2006) has an illuminating discussion on this.

69. <http://www.sudeepdiary.blogspot.com>, 11 October 2006, downloaded 6 June 2007.

70. 'Manipur Newspapers on Strike', *The Hindu*, 12 October 2007.

71. Anjulika Thingnam Samon, 'Manipur: The Tussle and the Compromise', *Infochange Agenda: Reporting Conflict*, Issue 14, 2009, p 13–17.

72. Discussion on Ratan Thiyyam's theatre is based on the following stories downloaded from e-pao.net on 7 December 2007; Atom Samarendra Singh, 'Ratan Thiyyam's Chorus Repertory Theatre'; Mindy Aloff, 'Together They Live, Work and Die'; and 'Contemporary Theatre Company from Manipur, India, presents *Nine Hills One Valley*', by Asia Society, New York.

73. 'Gladly Beyond Any Distance', blog by Anasuya, 2 May 2007.

74. Koubru—a lofty hill in the north-west corner of Manipur, a sacred place for many.

75. 'It is well known that up to the advent of Hinduism, the dead were buried, and the chronicles mentioned that Khagemba Maharajah enacted a rule to the effect that the dead were to be buried outside the enclosures of the houses. This was altered during the reign of Garib Niwaz. It is said that he exhumed the bones of his ancestors and cremated them on the bank of Engthi (Ningthi) river. Since then, he ordered his

subjects to burn their dead. This change took place sometime in the year 1724,' said T.C. Hudson (*The Meitheis*, 1908). Cited in Priyadarshini Gangte, 'Socio-cultural ties among the people of hills and plains', in *The Sangai Express*, 8 March 2007.

76. Irom Sharmila, in *Quarterly Journal*, ibid., p 93, translated by Tayenjam Bijoykumar Singh.

77. Ranabir Samaddar, 'Deaths, Responsibility and Justice', in Ranabir Samaddar, ed., *Peace Studies: An Introduction to the Concept, Scope and Themes* (New Delhi: Sage, 2004), p 151–172.

78. Johan Galtung, Carl G. Jacobsen and Kai Frithjof Brand-Jacobsen, *Searching for Peace: The Road to TRANSCEND* (London: Pluto Press, 2002), p xix.

79. Arambam Ongbi Memchoubi, *Quarterly Journal*, ibid., p 1–18.

80. Simon Fisher et al., *Working with Conflict—Skills and Strategies for Action* (London: Zed, 2000).

81. Bhagat Oinam, 'Dynamics of Ethnic Conflict in Manipur: Towards a Proposal for Solution' in Monirul Hasan, ed., *Coming Out of Violence: Essays on Ethnicity, Conflict Resolution and Peace Process in North-East India* (New Delhi: Regency Publications, 2005), p 127–140. Surinder S. Jodhka, ed., *Community and Identities—Contemporary Discourses on Culture and Politics in India* (New Delhi: Sage, 2001) also has relevant discussions, especially those by A.R. Vasavi and Satish Deshpande.

82. Khelena Gurumayum, *The Role of Manipuri Women in Crisis Management*, ibid., p 42, quoting from her interviews with R.K. Randhoni Devi on 21 May 2004; with Bimola Devi, member Kha Nongpok Nupi Lup on 21 May 2004; and with Taruni Devi, President of All Manipur Women's Social Reformation and Development Samaj, on 9 June 2004.

83. National Campaign Committee Against Militarisation and for Repeal of AFSPA, '*Where "Peacemakers" Have Declared War*', Report of a Seminar (New Delhi, 2007).

84. Gunjan Veda, ibid.

85. <http://www.worldpress.org> online features, 'The Merciless Killing of Thangjam Manorama', 23 July 2004, downloaded 14 July 2007.

86. Oinam Anand, 'Restoration of a Shrine: Past, Present and Future', *The Sangai Express*, e-pao.net, downloaded 23 July 2007.

87. Oinam Anand, ibid.

88. Kranti Kumar, ibid.

89. Bijo Francis, AHRC, 'Covenant of Civil and Political Rights', *Article 2*, p 13–26.

90. See Note 88.

91. Christel Stevens, 'Manipuri Laihui at Symphony Space', who saw a performance of Lai Haraoba in New York, notes wistfully, '... I certainly wished the whole audience could have followed the pathway right out into the streets of New York, to protect all the denizens from harmful influence for another year.' Webcast on 19 May 2007 on e-pao.net.

REFERENCES

The following list of books, journals and reports is by no means exhaustive. Many other documents were consulted in the course of the research. Most of the sources already mentioned in the endnotes have not been repeated here.

BOOKS, PAPERS AND CHAPTERS IN BOOKS

Brara, N. Vijayalakshmi, *A Situational Analysis of Women and Girls in Manipur*, New Delhi: National Commission for Women, 2005.

Chakravarti, Uma, 'The Burdens of Nationalism: Some Thoughts on South Asian Feminists and the Nation State', unpublished paper.

Dutta, Anuradha, and Ratna Bhuyan, ed., *Genesis of Conflict and Peace—Understanding Northeast India*. New Delhi: Akanksha Publishing House and OKDISCD, 2007.

Gandhi, M.K., *Non-violence in Peace and War*. Ahmedabad: Navajivan Publishing House, 1942.

Gill, Preeti, ed. *The Peripheral Centre: Voices from India's Northeast*. New Delhi: Zubaan, 2010.

Goshwami, Hareshwar, *History of the People of Manipur*. Imphal: Kangla Publications, 2004.

Gurumayum, Khelena, *The Role of Manipuri Women in Crisis Management during the Extension of Ceasefire between the Government of India and NSCN-IM without Territorial Limits*. New Delhi: WISCOMP, 2007.

Hussain, Monirul, ed., *Coming Out of Violence—Essays on Ethnicity, Conflict Resolution and Peace Process in North-East India*. New Delhi: Regency, 2005.

Kabui, Gangmumei, *History of Manipur, Vol. 1: Pre-Colonial Period*. New Delhi: National Publishing House, 1991.

Khala, Khatoli, *The Armed Forces (Special Powers) Act and Its Impact on Women in Nagaland*. New Delhi: WISCOMP, 2003.

Manchanda, Rita, ed., *Women, War and Peace in South Asia: Beyond Victimhood to Agency*. New Delhi: Sage, 2001.

Mehrotra, Deepti Priya, 'Irom Sharmila's Protest Fast: "Women's Wars", Gandhian Non-Violence and Anti-Militarisation Struggles', Peace Prints: South Asian Journal of Peacebuilding, Vol. 3, No.1: Spring 2010, WISCOMP.

Mehrotra, Deepti Priya, 'Restoring Order in Manipur: The Drama of Contemporary Women's Protests', in Gill, Preeti, ed. *The Peripheral Centre: Voices from India's Northeast*. New Delhi: Zubaan, 2010.

Mohanty, Aparna, ed., *Human Rights and Women of Northeast India*. Dibrugarh: Centre for Women's Studies, Dibrugarh University, 2002.

Nojeim, Michael J., *Gandhi and King: The Power of Non-violent Resistance*. Praeger, 2004.

Rammohan, E.N., *Insurgent Frontiers: Essays from the Troubled Northeast*. New Delhi: India Research Press, 2005.

Ratan Kumar, *Lai Haraoba of Manipur*. Imphal: Pratima Devi, 2001.

Sanajaoba, Naorem, ed., *Manipur Past and Present—The Ordeals and Heritage of a Civilisation*. New Delhi: Mittal, 1991.

Shankar, Charu, 'Timeless in Imphal', *The Dance of Life*, Vol. IV, Issue 5, February–March 2007.

Sharmila, Irom, *Frangrance of Peace*. New Delhi: Zubaan, 2010.

Sharmila, Irom and Vaid, Minnie, *Iron Irom: Two Journeys*. New Delhi: Rajpal and Sons, 2013.

Singh, O. Kulabidhu, *Sharmila: A Mission for Peace*. Imphal: Oinam Ongbi Gulapmachu Devi, 2006.

Singh, R.K. Jhalajit, *A History of Manipuri Literature*. Imphal: Manipur University, 1976, Second Edition 1987.

Takhellambum, Bhabananda, *Women's Uprising in Manipur: A Legacy Continued*. New Delhi: WISCOMP, 2003.

Tarapot, Phanjoubam, *Bleeding Manipur*. New Delhi: Har-Anand, 2004.

Veda, Gunjan, *Tailoring Peace: The Citizens' Roundtable on Manipur and Beyond*. Guwahati: North East Network, 2005.

Yamini Devi, *Parvat ke Paar*, a collection of short stories, translated from Manipuri to Hindi by Elaibam Vijaylakshmi. Imphal: Rai Praveena Brothers, 2005.

REPORTS, JOURNALS AND ARTICLES

Amnesty International India, 'Briefing: The Armed Forces Special Powers Act: A Renewed Debate in India on Human Rights and National Security'. September 2013. Accessed at www.amnestyusa.org, on 25.9.2014.

Dobhal, Harsh, ed., *Manipur in the Shadow of AFSPA: Independent People's Tribunal on Torture, Extra-judicial Executions and Forced Disappearances*. New Delhi: Human Rights Law Network, December 2009.

Human Rights Watch, 'These Fellows Must Be Eliminated: Relentless Violence and Impunity in Manipur'. New York: Human Rights Watch, 2008.

'The Report of the Committee on Amendments to Criminal Law', Government of India. Committee led by retired Justice J.S. Verma. New Delhi: 23 January 2013.

Ninthouja, Malem, ed. *Armed Forces Special Powers Act, 1958: Manipur Experience,* Campaign for Peace and Democracy (Manipur), New Delhi: 2010.

Commission of Inquiry, Justice Santosh Hegde Commission Report, 'Extrajudicial Killings in Manipur'. Government of India: 4 April 2013.

Quarterly Journal, No. 23, Manipuri Women on a New Role. Imphal: Manipur State Kala Akademi, February 2007.

'*Covenant of Civil and Political Rights*', *Article 2 of the International Covenant on Civil and Political Rights, Special edition on Militarisation and Impunity in Manipur*, Vol. 5, No. 6, December 2006, p 35–37.

Mehrotra, Deepti Priya, 'Daughter of Peace', Indpendent World Report, Issue 2, November 2009.

Report of Commission on Human Rights, Fifty-ninth Session. Geneva: Economic and Social Council, UNESCO, 2003.

Political Movements and Nationality Question in Northeast India—A Report. Delhi: Manipur Research Forum, 2006.

National Campaign Committee Against Militarisation and for Repeal of AFSPA, '*Where "Peacemakers" Have Declared War*'. New Delhi: Report of a Seminar, 2007.

Accords, Peace Processes and Prospects of Civil Society Peace Initiatives. Guwahati: North East Peace Initiatives, 2007.

Press Information Bureau, Defence Wing, 'Annual Report—Army in the Northeast', from e-pao.net, webcast on 16 November 2006.

Review of AFSPA 1958, Justice Jeevan Reddy Committee Report. New Delhi: unpublished, 2005.

The AFSPA: Lawless Law Enforcement According to the Law? Asian Centre for Human Rights, 21 January 2005.

An Analysis of Armed Forces Special Powers Act, 1958. PUCL Bulletin, March 2005.

India: Time to Repeal the Armed Forces Special Powers Act. Amenesty International Public Statement, 10 July 2006.

Joshi, Sandeep, 'Army's stand makes it hard to amend AFSPA: Chidambaram.' *The Hindu*, 2013.